Unbuildable Tatlin?!
Edited by Klaus Bollinger,
Florian Medicus, IoA

**Head of the Institute of
Architecture:** Wolf D. Prix
Editors in Chief: Roswitha Janowski-
Fritsch, Florian Medicus
Translation: Wolfgang Dallasera,
Camilla Nielsen
Proof reading: Camilla Nielsen
Design: Atelier Dreibholz
Printing: Holzhausen Druck GmbH

Printed on acid-free and chlorine-free
bleached paper

© 2012 Springer-Verlag/Wien

Printed in Austria

SpringerWienNewYork is a part of
Springer Science + Business Media
springer.at

SPIN: 12594818

With over 100 Figures

ISSN 1866-248X
ISBN 978-3-211-99201-2

SpringerWienNewYork

 **INSTITUTE OF
ARCHITECTURE**

edition: ˈʌŋgevʌndtə

Edition Angewandte
Book Series of the University of
Applied Arts Vienna
Edited by Gerald Bast, Rector

Unbuildable Tatlin?!

Edited by Klaus Bollinger and Florian Medicus

SpringerWienNewYork

Recreation of Tatlin's Tower in the Royal Academy's courtyard 2011–12. Photo: Courtesy of Francis Ware

Contents

7 **Foreword: The Courage to Cross Boundaries**
Gerald Bast

10 *The Great Utopia*
Zaha Hadid

General section
14 **Tatlin**
Klaus Bollinger

28 **Miscellanea of Ingenious Architecture in the Soviet Avant-Garde**
Frank Rolf Werner

Specific section
46 **The Work Awaiting Us**
V. Y. Tatlin, T. Shapiro, I. Meyerzon, P. Vinogradov

51 **Tatlin's Tower, Vision and Pretension, from 1917 onwards**
Florian Medicus

67 **The Curved Line as Form, Metaphor, and Policy**
Gabriele Werner

76 **The Theory of Spirals**
Georg Glaeser

About the seminar
86 **Unbuildable Tatlin?!**
Klaus Bollinger, Wilfried Braumüller, Florian Medicus, 2007

95 **Geometric Reconstruction with Poor-Quality Photos**
Franz Gruber

102 **About the Seminar "Unbuildable Tatlin?!"**
Florian Medicus, Kurt Polanec, 2009

124 **Final Presentation**

128 **Vladimir Tatlin, Biography**

Inhalt

7 **Vorwort: Vom Mut Grenzen zu überschreiten**
Gerald Bast

10 *Die Große Utopie*
Zaha Hadid

Allgemeiner Teil
14 **Tatlin**
Klaus Bollinger

28 **Miszellen zu ingeniösen Architekturen zuzeiten der sowjetischen Avantgarde**
Frank Rolf Werner

Spezieller Teil
46 **Die Arbeit, die uns erwartet**
W. J. Tatlin, T. Schapiro, I. Meierson, P. Winogradow

51 **Tatlins Turm, Vision und Anmaßung, 1917ff.**
Florian Medicus

67 **Die gekrümmte Linie als Form, Metapher und Politik**
Gabriele Werner

76 **Spiralentheorie**
Georg Glaeser

Zum Seminar
86 **Unbuildable Tatlin?!**
Klaus Bollinger, Wilfried Braumüller, Florian Medicus, 2007

95 **Geometrische Rekonstruktion basierend auf Fotos schlechter Bildqualität**
Franz Gruber

102 **Zum Seminar »Unbuildable Tatlin?!«**
Florian Medicus, Kurt Polanec, 2009

124 **Abschlusspräsentation**

128 **Wladimir Tatlin, Biografie**

Model of The Tower, Moderna Museet, Stockholm

Foreword: The Courage to Cross Boundaries

Gerald Bast

Vorwort: Vom Mut Grenzen zu überschreiten

Gerald Bast

Boundaries are here to be crossed! An old sentimental socio-revolutionary approach endorsed by artists? Well, there are many artists who reject this social and political mission of art, claiming that art has to be free, also vis-à-vis society. Looking back in history, one is often pleasantly surprised to see that the opposite is true—artists being intimately bound to their work, society and their reality. It is not about...

The Russian painter, constructivist and avant-garde artist Vladimir Tatlin was one of them. In 1919 he designed the enormous tower made of glass and steel. The tower was supposed to be the symbol of social revolution in Russia and to resemble a huge machine, true to its motto: "Art is dead. Long live the new machine art ..." Precisely this vision, at the time very revolutionary, provides a nice illustration of the utopian power of art to change society which artists can offer.

Grenzen sind dazu da, überschritten zu werden! Ein alter, sentimentaler, von KünstlerInnen vertretener gesellschafts-revolutionärer Ansatz?

Nun – viele KünstlerInnen weisen diesen gesellschaftlichen, wie auch den politischen Auftrag der Künste zurück und meinen, Kunst müsse frei sein, auch gegenüber ihrer Gesellschaft. Der Rückblick in die Geschichte zeigt aber immer wieder erfrischend das Gegenteil, nämlich den engen Bezug und die Verwobenheit von KünstlerInnen mit ihrer Kunst, Gesellschaft und ihrer Wirklichkeit. Es geht nicht ...

Der russische Maler, Konstruktivist und Avantgarde Künstler Wladimir Tatlin war einer von ihnen. Er entwarf 1919 einen gigantischen Glas-Stahl-Turm. Der Turm sollte das Symbol für die soziale Revolution in Russland werden und einer riesigen Maschine gleichen, getreu seinem Motto: »Die Kunst ist tot. Es lebe die neue

This power was so powerful that decades later the American light artist Dan Flavin cited Tatlin's monument in the 39 sculptures of his series titled "monuments to V. Tatlin". This series, created between 1964 and 1990, called into question the human need for huge monuments, linking Tatlin's concept with a main symbol of capitalism but also honouring the political visions of the constructivist.

Ai Weiwei, the Chinese concept artist, also addressed Tatlin's vision when he created his piece "Fountain of Light" in 2007.

Now that art has become autonomous and no longer stands in the service of Western and religious rulers, it is less true than ever that art and artists are completely outside of all social systems. This is especially true for architecture—society has an effect on art and vice versa—also and often precisely when the opposite claim is made. There is hardly any other place where the interactions between art and society, the connections and contradictions between the prevailing aesthetic and technological zeitgeist and the desire for the novel becomes so clearly visible as in architecture. That contemporary artists in particular take up Tatlin's ideas and quote them for their own purposes underlines the theory that artists and art-minded people contribute in a positive and visionary way to the further development of society. Art is never an end-in-itself, completely detached from society, never "l'art pour l'art" in an everyday sense but rather a point of departure and a means of communication in society—having an effect either on preserving the existing or for developing and further developing art and thus also society in which it is rooted.

Maschinenkunst ...«. Gerade diese, für die damalige Zeit revolutionäre Vision, veranschaulicht sehr schön die gesellschafts-verändernde utopistische Kraft, die von KünstlerInnen ausgehen kann.

Diese Kraft wirkt so stark, dass Jahrzehnte später der amerikanische Lichtkünstler Dan Flavin Tatlins Monument in den 39 Skulpturen seiner Serie »monuments to V. Tatlin« zitiert. Diese zwischen 1964 und 1990 entstandene Serie, die das menschliche Bedürfnis nach großen Denkmälern hinterfragt, brachte so Tatlins Konzept mit einem Hauptsymbol des Kapitalismus in Verbindung, würdigte aber auch die politischen Visionen des Konstruktivisten. Auch der chinesische Konzeptkünstler Ai Weiwei nimmt Tatlins Vision auf und kreiert 2007 sein Werk »Fountain of Light«.

Die Autonomisierung der Kunst, als Befreiung von Aufträgen im Dienste weltlicher und religiöser Herrscher bedeutet heute weniger denn je, dass die Kunst und die KünstlerInnen außerhalb jeglicher sozialer Systeme stehen würden. Das gilt für die Baukunst in ganz besonderem Maße. Die Gesellschaft wirkt auf die Kunst ein und umgekehrt – auch und oft gerade dann, wenn das Gegenteil behauptet wird. Kaum wo sonst werden die Wechselwirkungen zwischen Kunst und Gesellschaft, die Zusammenhänge und Widersprüche zwischen einem herrschenden ästhetischen und technologischen Zeitgeist einerseits und die Sehnsucht nach Neuem so deutlich sichtbar wie in der Architektur. Dass gerade Künstler der Gegenwart die Ideen von Tatlin aufgreifen und für ihre Zwecke als Beleg zitieren, unterstreicht die These, dass KünstlerInnen und künstlerisch denkende Menschen dazu beitragen, Gesellschaften in

That this is not happening in a trivial or mechanist sense is something everyone is aware of—except perhaps for the propagators of a modern "Biedermeier" style.

visionärer Weise positiv weiterzuentwickeln. Kunst ist nie gesellschaftsfreier Selbstzweck, nie »l'art pour l'art« im umgangssprachlich kolportierten Sinne, sondern ganz wesentlich Ausgangspunkt und Medium zur Kommunikation in der Gesellschaft – entweder zur Bewahrung des Seienden oder für die Entwicklung und Weiterentwicklung der Kunst und damit der Gesellschaft, in der sie steht. Dass dies nicht in einer trivial-mechanistischen Form geschieht wissen alle – außer vielleicht die Propagandisten des modernen Biedermeier.

Reconstruction of Tatlin's *Complex Corner Relief*, 1915 by Martyn Chalk

The Great Utopia

Zaha Hadid

Die Große Utopie

Zaha Hadid

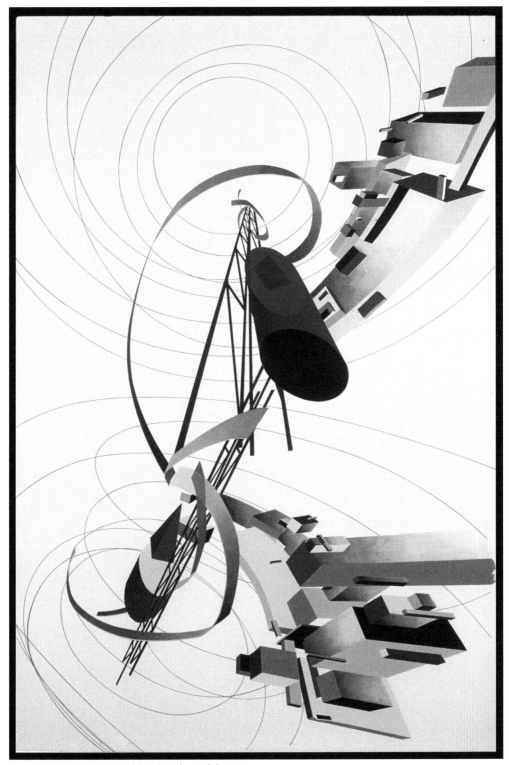

Tatlin Tower and Tectonic "Worldwind", Zaha Hadid, 1992

The Great Utopia

General section

Allgemeiner Teil

Tatlin

Klaus Bollinger

Tatlin

Klaus Bollinger

The "Unbuildable Tatlin?!" seminar was a fascinating experience for all participants. What fascinated me personally? I guess it was the understanding of utopia, not as an unattainable counter-model but as a set goal within reach. Conventions and standards, including technical ones, were questioned in an environment that was, at that time, open. Everything was possible; everything was achievable, even the dream of flying. Later in the 1930s, Tatlin demanded that every Soviet citizen their own private flying apparatus for. The dream of flying goes hand in hand with the dream of defying gravity. Buildings seemingly grow towards the sky against the laws of physics; they appear as floating bars or as tribunes that are no longer vertical but tilt towards the viewer in the form of skewed cantilever, as though gravity did not exist. Alongside the (virtual) negation of existing laws, these gestures are

Das Seminar »Unbuildable Tatlin?!« war für alle Beteiligten eine faszinierende Erfahrung. Was hat mich persönlich fasziniert dabei? Es ist dieses Verständnis von Utopie. Nicht als unerreichbares Gegenmodell, sondern anzustrebendes Ziel, das in erreichbarer Nähe ist. Konventionen und Standards, auch technische Standards, wurden in dem damaligen offenen Umfeld in Frage gestellt. Alles war möglich, alles war erreichbar. Bis hin zur Verwirklichung des Traums vom Fliegen: Tatlin forderte später in den 1930er Jahren den eigenen Flugapparat für jeden Sowjetbürger. Der Traum vom Fliegen geht einher mit dem Traum von der Aufhebung der Gravitation. Gebäude wachsen scheinbar gegen die Gesetze der Physik in die Höhe, sie sind vermeintlich schwebende Riegel oder die Rednertribüne steht nicht senkrecht, sondern neigt sich als schräger Kragarm dem Publikum zu, als würde die Gravitation nicht

also an expression of social dynamics—like the spiral in Tatlin's monument.

The specifications of El Lissitzky's *Wolkenbügel* reflect the belief in development and foresight at that time. "The skeleton is made of new types of non-rusting and high tensile steels (from Krupp). Materials for the internal walls and floors should be light and highly insulating with regards to thermal and sound transmission. The glass is chemically processed to permit the transmission of light but to obstruct heat rays.

Here techniques and materials that were not yet available in the still industrially undeveloped Soviet Union are described. But the foresight of those years has for us become self-evident reality.

Belief in the ability of engineering was strengthened by figures such as Vladimir Shukhov. By the end of the nineteenth century, Shukhov had already invented and built ingenious constructions. His buildings remain a treasure trove of innovative constructions up to this day. Among them are frame shells, suspended roofs, the roof of the GUM department store and, last but not least, his radio tower, which was supposed to dwarf the Eiffel Tower (1889) while weighing considerably less. Due to the lack of steel, unfortunately, only a smaller version of the radio tower was built.

The idea that utopia can become reality defined the spirit of those years. And it was important for our students to show how it could be implemented now and/or then. What we support at the Institute of Architecture at the University of Applied Arts is an openness of thought in the utopian sense. Thus ideas that can be implemented with today's means ought to be

existieren. Neben der (scheinbaren) Negation bestehender Gesetze sind diese Gesten auch Ausdruck der gesellschaftlichen Dynamik – wie die Spirale des Tatlin-Monumentes.

Ein Bild von dem damaligen Glauben in den Fortschritt und die Weitsicht (Weitsichtigkeit ist medizinisch) gibt die Baubeschreibung zu El Lissitzkys Wolkenbügel: »Das Gerüst besteht aus neuartigem rostfreien, hochfestem Stahl (von Krupp). Die für die Innenwände und Böden verwendeten Baustoffe sollten leicht sein und eine hohe Isolierung gegen Wärme und Schall bieten. Das Glas wurde chemisch bearbeitet, um die Übertragung von Licht zu ermöglichen bzw. das Eindringen von Wärmestrahlen zu blockieren.«

Hier werden Techniken und Materialien beschrieben, die in der damaligen industriell noch nicht entwickelten Sowjetunion so noch nicht verfügbar waren. Aber aus der damaligen weitsichtigen Vision ist für uns heute selbstverständliche Wirklichkeit geworden.

Der Glaube an die Möglichkeiten der Ingenieure wurde auch bestärkt durch Persönlichkeiten wie Wladimir Šuchov. Šuchov hat bereits Ende des 19. Jahrhunderts geniale Konstruktionen erfunden und gebaut. Seine Bauten stellen heute für uns noch eine Fundgrube innovativer Konstruktionen dar. Darunter sind Stabwerkschalen, Hängedächer, das Dach des Kaufhauses GUM und nicht zuletzt der Radioturm, der den Eiffelturm (1889) an Höhe übertreffen, aber an Leichtigkeit weit unterbieten sollte. Aus Mangel an Stahl konnte jedoch nur eine kleinere Variante gebaut werden.

Die Utopie ist machbar, das war der Geist jener Jahre. Und es war für

developed, but so too should ideas that are experimental and pointing towards the future. At the same time, we want to encourage students to find possible solutions for the implementation of seemingly utopian designs.

In our practical work, we see that many projects that were deemed utopian only a few years ago are considered normal today. We therefore always have to move forward and open up new fields. I would like to highlight this with a few examples from our work.

BMW Welt Munich, Coop Himmelb(l)au

Today we are able to work on even very complex supporting structures with the aid of digital technology. Thus a system of supporting structures does not have to be broken down into separate parts to be calculated. Instead a whole system, with all its elements and interactions, can be examined.

A special challenge of this project was the development and construction of a roof measuring 200 × 120 m, supported by the building's existing elements and only a few additional columns. Parallel to the design of the model at Coop Himmelb(l)au, we digitally developed the geometry of the freely formed roof with the aid of a framework program. Two initially flat, flexible layers of girder grid with a norm grid of 5 × 5 m were shaped by virtual load scenarios. The upper girder grid was arched upwards in the form of a cushion by negative gravitation, while virtual forces, derived from the areas and structures below, were applied on the lower grid. The connection with diagonal trusses results

die Studierenden wichtig, im Rahmen des Seminars die damalige und/oder heutige Umsetzbarkeit aufzuzeigen. Was wir am Institut für Architektur an der Universität für Angewandte Kunst fördern, ist die Offenheit des Denkens im Sinne von Utopien. Damit sollen einerseits Ideen entwickelt werden, die mit den heutigen Mitteln bereits umsetzbar sind. Es sollen auch Ideen entwickelt werden, welche eher Forschungscharakter haben können, indem sie Wege für die Zukunft aufzeigen. Gleichzeitig wollen wir die Studierenden anregen, auch die Möglichkeiten für die Realisierung scheinbar utopischer Entwürfe zu entdecken.

In unserer praktischen Arbeit sehen wir, dass das, was vor wenigen Jahren noch als utopisch galt, heute selbstverständlich ist. Deshalb müssen wir uns immer wieder weiterbewegen und neue Felder erschließen. Das möchte ich im Folgenden mit einigen Beispielen aus unserer Arbeit zeigen.

BMW Welt München, Coop Himmelb(l)au

Wir sind heute in der Lage, mittels digitaler Techniken auch sehr komplexe Tragwerke zu bearbeiten. Man muss ein Tragwerkssystem also nicht mehr zwangsläufig in seine Einzelteile zerlegen, um es berechnen zu können. Stattdessen wird das gesamte System mit all seinen Elementen und deren Interaktionen untersucht.

Eine besondere Herausforderung war die Entwicklung und Konstruktion des Daches mit seiner Ausdehnung von 200 × 120 m, getragen von den vorhandenen Bauteilen und nur wenigen zusätzlichen Stützen. Parallel zum Entwurf am Modell bei Coop Himmelb(l)au haben wir mithilfe eines Stabwerksprogrammes die Geometrie

BMW Welt: Interior view of the Double Cone made of steel and glass

South entrance of BMW Welt. A pedestrian bridge leads to the second level of the building, past the dynamic Double Cone.

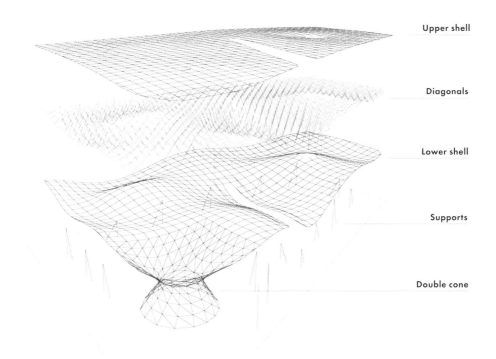

Upper shell

Diagonals

Lower shell

Supports

Double cone

BMW Welt: Exploded view of structural elements

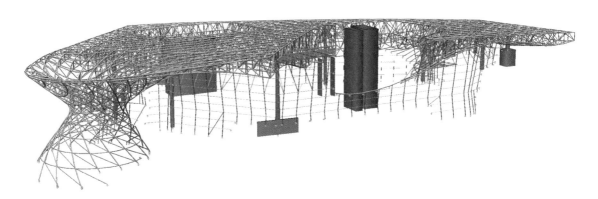

BMW Welt: Isometric view, structure

Unbuildable Tatlin?!

in a highly effective spatial supporting structure. The roof was also deformed against the backdrop of a well-conceived supporting structure system, where the different heights of the structure were adapted to the individual loads. Thus we developed a mixed system combining different local behaviors. One example is the girder grid of the BMW roof, the bending resistance effect of which gradually yields to the shell-like supporting effect of the double cone.

Rolex Learningcenter, SANAA

On the grounds of the École Polytechnique Fédérale (EPFL) in Lausanne, the so-called Rolex Learning Center was completed in 2010. A single-storey building with a rectangular layout of 121.5 × 162.5 m, it was designed by SANAA, the Japanese office of Kazuyo Sejima and Ryue Nishizawa. In many areas, the building rises up in the form of waves like a rippled carpet. In doing so, the lifted ground panel bridges span lengths of up to 80 m. The form does not strictly follow the principles or behavior of a purely shell-like supporting structure. The challenge was to realize the shell's load-bearing capacity without introducing additional columns. With this "utopia" as a goal, numerous alternative forms of construction were examined and comprehensive arithmetical verifications conducted in various models and programs. The result is a 60 cm thick steel and concrete shell with reinforcements of up to 80 cm in some areas.

Hungerburgbahn, Zaha Hadid

At the end of 2007, the Hungerburgbahn, designed by Zaha Hadid, was inaugurated.

des frei verformten Daches direkt digital entwickelt. Es wurden zwei zunächst ebene, biegeweiche Trägerrostlagen mit einem Regelraster von 5 × 5 m durch fiktive Lastszenarien verformt. Der obere Trägerrost wurde durch negative Gravitation kissenförmig nach oben gewölbt, auf den unteren Rost wurden fiktive Kräfte aufgebracht, die aus den darunter liegenden Flächen und Baukörpern hergeleitet wurden. Durch die Verbindung mit diagonalen Streben entsteht ein Raumtragwerk mit hoher Effizienz. Die Verformung des Daches erfolgte auch vor dem Hintergrund einer sinnvollen Tragwerksentwicklung. Die unterschiedlichen Höhen des Tragwerks sind an die jeweilige Beanspruchung angepasst. So entstand quasi ein Mischsystem mit lokal unterschiedlichem Verhalten, wie der Trägerrost des BMW-Daches, dessen Biegetragwirkung graduell in eine schalenähnliche Tragwirkung des Doppelkegels übergeht.

Rolex Learningcenter, SANAA

Auf dem Gelände der École Polytechnique Fédérale (EPFL) in Lausanne wurde 2010 das sogenannte Rolex Learning Center fertig gestellt. Die eingeschossige architektonische Landschaft steht auf einer Grundfläche von 121,5 × 162,5 m. Das Gebäude löst sich in weiten Bereichen wellenartig vom Boden wie ein aufgeschobener Teppich. Die abgehobene Bodenplatte überbrückt dabei freie Spannweiten bis zu 80 m. Die so von SANAA entwickelte Form folgt nicht streng den Gesetzmäßigkeiten, die ein reines Schalentragverhalten zur Folge haben kann. Die Herausforderung bestand darin, die Tragfähigkeit der Schale zu realisieren, ohne dass zusätzliche Stützen eingeführt werden

Rolex Learning Center, Lausanne (rendering)

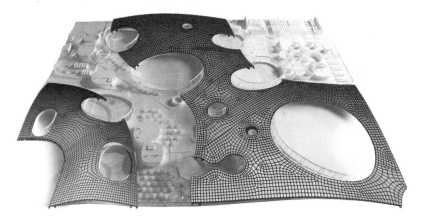

Rolex Learning Center: Meshes of the finite element models of the big and the small shell

Rolex Learning Center: Big shell after removing of the formwork

It is a rail-bound mountain railway with four stops and differently designed roofs.

Bollinger + Grohmann developed the complete planning of the supporting framework for Pagitz, the executing company. An interior steel construction simultaneously supports and gives form by providing the direct support for the double-curved glass panels. Steel frames are arranged in a grid at 1.25 m, the outer shape of which exactly follows the enveloping area at a distance of 60 mm. Longitudinal ribs are welded between the lateral ribs, resulting in a girder grid of iron sheets up to 3 meters tall.

To ensure a cost-effective assembly and also minimize the necessary blueprints, the main assembly information was drawn directly onto the steel plates. To facilitate the control of the CNC machines, the outer edges of each station's steel elements were drawn in a 3D-model from which the geometry for automated production could be directly derived.

The plane outer hull consists of 1100 glass panels. Each element is a unique double-curved copy, produced manually from a distinctive negative form made from bent steel pipes and checked by a 3D-scanner before delivery.

Generation of Supporting Structures

The potential of digital technologies is not only limited to use as a tool in the framework of technical drawing and production, but also enables a limitless generation of forms and structures. Analytical and simulation software give planners today a whole range of tools that allow for the evolutionary development of entire populations of supporting structures

mussten. Mit dieser »Utopie« vor Augen wurden zahlreiche Konstruktionsalternativen untersucht und umfassende rechnerische Nachweise mit unterschiedlichen Modellen und Programmen geführt. Das Ergebnis ist eine 60 cm dicke Stahlbetonschale mit bereichsweise angeordneten Verstärkungen auf 80 cm.

Hungerburgbahn, Zaha Hadid

2007 wurde die Hungerburgbahn nach den Plänen von Zaha Hadid eröffnet. Es handelt sich um eine schienengebundene Bergbahn mit vier Haltestellen und unterschiedlich ausgeführten Dächern.

Bollinger+Grohmann hat die gesamte Tragwerksplanung der Dächer für die ausführende Firma Pagitz entwickelt. Eine innere Stahlkonstruktion bildet sowohl das Tragwerk als auch die formgebende Struktur, indem sie das direkte Auflager für die zweisinnig gekrümmten Glasscheiben bildet. Im Raster von 1,25 m sind Stahlspanten angeordnet, deren Außenkontur mit 60 mm Abstand exakt der Hüllfläche folgt. Zwischen diese Querspanten sind Längsspanten geschweißt, so dass ein Trägerrost aus bis zu 3 m hohen Blechen entsteht.

Um eine kostengünstige Montage zu ermöglichen und um die Anzahl der benötigten Werkzeichnungen zu minimieren, wurden die wesentlichen Informationen für den Zusammenbau direkt auf die Stahlplatten gezeichnet. Als Grundlage für die Steuerung der CNC-Maschinen wurde von jeder Station ein 3D-Modell der Außenkanten der Stahlelemente gezeichnet, aus denen die Geometrie für die automatisierte Fertigung direkt abgeleitet werden konnte.

that are tested for their capability in an architectonical context where only the fittest survive. Next to the graphical interface, these applications also offer a programming or scripting interface, allowing for an automation of rule-based processes.

We did our first experiments in a project in Naples (together with the architect Dominique Perrault). The entrance to the Stazione Metropolitana Linea 1, with a connected mall, will be located on the first basement floor. This carved trench is to be connected to the square above by a roof that grows out of the trench.

Since the possibility of a folded plate was discussed early in the process, we tried to generate a folded plate based on triangles at the computer. We started out with a plane surface, and then a special program was used to lift and lower points at random. Some of these points could bear, while others did not. A simple fitness criterion was the maximum deflection at which separation into different variants was possible. This begins with a random generation, after which variants are evaluated and combined in pairs. Thus a new generation with enhanced characteristics develops. To make the random process even more diverse, individual variants can be subjected to mutations as they transform into new forms. The richness of variants soon leads to a convergence. Variants optimized with regards to specific characteristics emerge. They are all similar but never the same.

We also used this procedure in other projects. Coop Himmelb(l)au developed a box with a special roof for an aquarium in Vienna. This roof required openings, some of which were to be permeable and some

Die glatte Außenhülle besteht aus 1100 Glaspaneelen. Jedes einzelne Element ist ein zweisinnig gekrümmtes Unikat, welches jeweils durch eine eigene Negativform aus gebogenen Stahlrohren manuell hergestellt und vor der Auslieferung mit einem 3D-Scanner kontrolliert wurde.

Tragwerksgenerierung

Das Potential digitaler Technologien beschränkt sich jedoch nicht auf den Einsatz als Werkzeug im Rahmen der Darstellungstechnik und der Produktion, sondern es ermöglicht auch eine fast uneingeschränkte Generierung von Formen und Strukturen. Analyse- und Simulationssoftware stellen den Planern heute Werkzeuge zur Verfügung, die ganze Populationen von Tragwerken evolutionär entwickeln lassen, indem ihre Leistungsfähigkeit im architektonischen Kontext auf die Probe gestellt wird und nur die fittesten Individuen überleben. So bieten diese Anwendungen neben der grafischen Oberfläche eine Programmier- oder Scripting-Schnittstelle, die es erlaubt, regelbasierte Prozesse zu automatisieren.

Erste Versuche dazu haben wir bei einem Projekt in Neapel (Architekt: Dominique Perrault) gemacht. Der Eingang zur Stazione Metropolitana Linea 1 mit angeschlossener Mall wird über das erste Untergeschoss erfolgen. Dieser eingeschnittene Graben soll mit einem aus ihm heraus wachsenden Dach mit dem darüber liegenden Platz verbunden werden.

Bereits früh wurde in diesem Zusammenhang über die Möglichkeit eines Faltwerks diskutiert. Wir haben am Computer den Versuch unternommen, ein Faltwerk aus Dreiecken zu generieren. Wir begannen mit

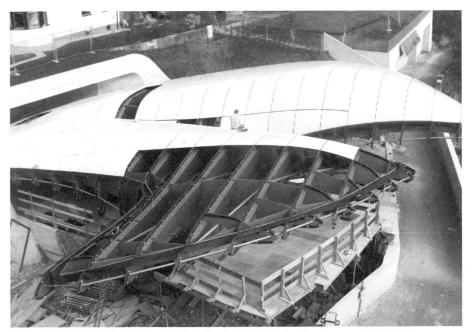

Hungerburgbahn by Zaha Hadid, Hungerburg Station under construction

Hungerburgbahn by Zaha Hadid, Hungerburg Station

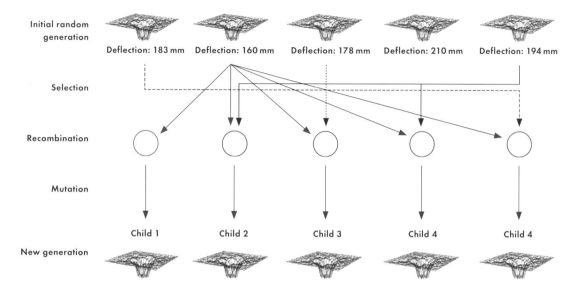

| Initial random generation | | | | |
| Deflection: 183 mm | Deflection: 160 mm | Deflection: 178 mm | Deflection: 210 mm | Deflection: 194 mm |

Selection

Recombination

Mutation

| Child 1 | Child 2 | Child 3 | Child 4 | Child 4 |

New generation

Underground station roof, Piazza Garibaldi, Naples, Dominique Perrault, Italy 2007, evolutionary process

Underground station roof, Piazza Garibaldi, Naples, Dominique Perrault, Italy 2007, competition model

tight. The basic given form was a distorted cone, which was to be self-supporting towards the interior box. After setting points on the building, we made the program place columns according to an evolutionary process, first with the presetting of minimal deflections. In the second step, the openings were generated automatically. Here, the combined criterion was made up of an average maximum deflection and the local deflection. As a final step, the height of the supporting shapes was adapted automatically to the static loads and thus optimized.

It is possible to control a parametric model with complex hierarchies and dependencies by changing the input parameters of this first generation. If these parameters have not been assigned variable values, a number of geometrically different derivations can be generated through manipulation of them. The use of parametric software enables one to design and also describe a process of generation in addition to the final object, thus offering a parametric spectrum of possible solutions.

The Milan architect Mario Bellini designed a sculpture for the lobby of the main headquarters of the Deutsche Bank. This sculpture resembles a sphere wrapped in bands, which connects the two towers of the Deutsche Bank.

The idea of wrapping was further refined after the competition in close collaboration with the architect. A series of sixty rings with varying radiuses is placed on the surface of a virtual sphere. The arrangement of the rings was supposed to be as even as possible, suspended without additional supporting structures and not penetrating the air space profiles of two bridges passing through them.

einer ebenen Fläche, danach ließen wir ein spezielles Programm die Punkte nach einem Zufallsprinzip heben und senken. Manche Zufallsprodukte trugen, manche nicht. Ein einfaches Fitnesskriterium war dabei die maximale Durchbiegung, nach dem man die verschiedenen Varianten trennen konnte.

Durch Veränderung der Eingabeparameter dieser ersten Generation kann somit ein parametrisches Modell mit komplexen Hierarchien und Abhängigkeiten gesteuert werden. Sind diese Parameter nicht mit variablen Werten belegt, können durch ihre Manipulation eine Vielzahl von geometrisch unterschiedlichen Ableitungen erzeugt werden. Beim Verwenden von parametrischer Software entwirft und beschreibt man also neben dem fertigen Objekt immer auch seinen Bildungsprozess und damit eine parametrische Bandbreite möglicher Lösungen. Statt einer einzelnen Lösung erhält man einen Raum mit vielen möglichen Lösungen.

Für das Foyer des Hauptsitzes der Deutschen Bank entwarf der Mailänder Architekt Mario Bellini eine Skulptur, die einer mit Bändern umwickelten Sphäre gleicht, die die beiden Türme der Deutschen Bank verbindet.

Die Idee der Wicklung wurde nach dem Wettbewerb in enger Zusammenarbeit mit dem Architekten weiterentwickelt. Eine Serie von 60 Ringen mit unterschiedlichen Radien wird auf der virtuellen Sphärenoberfläche platziert. Die Anordnung der Ringe sollte möglichst gleichmäßig sein, ohne zusätzliche Tragstrukturen frei spannen und die Luftraumprofile zweier, sie durchdringender Brücken, nicht durchstoßen.

Im ersten Schritt wurden sechzig Kreise erzeugt, die stets durch drei Punkte

As a first step sixty circles were generated which were defined by three points on the surface of the sphere. The coordinates of these circles—the parameters of the model—represented the genome for the genetic algorithm and were later subject to manipulation.

An optimum load-bearing structure could have been created by suspending the arches between the free supports. Such a configuration, however, would have had too many rings on similar levels so that the rings would have been distributed unevenly. The genetic algorithm assesses each individual on the sphere on the basis of all criteria so that solutions emerge which can do justice to all requirements. This approach ensures a large spectrum of variants and prevents a local optimum from being identified as a best solution. The development process ends when pre-defined limit values have been attained in the service of fitness.

Just as today a computer can naturally generate forms, it can be expected that what was once a utopia—automatically generated and optimized supporting structures—will soon become reality.

auf der Sphärenoberfläche definiert waren. Die Koordinaten dieser Kreise – die Parameter des Modells – stellten das Genom für den genetischen Algorithmus dar und waren im späteren Verlauf Gegenstand von Manipulation.

Die beste Tragwerkslösung entstünde durch das Spannen von Bögen zwischen dem Auflagern. Eine solche Konfiguration hätte jedoch viele Ringe in ähnlichen Ebenen, so dass es zu einer unregelmäßigen Verteilung der Ringe gekommen wäre. Der genetische Algorithmus bewertet jedoch jedes Sphärenindividuum auf Grundlage aller Kriterien gleichzeitig, so dass sich Lösungen herausbilden, die allen Anforderungen gerecht werden und eine Balance zwischen ihnen herstellen. Diese Vorgehensweise stellt eine große Bandbreite von Varianten sicher und verhindert, dass ein lokales Optimum als vermeintlich beste Lösung identifiziert wird. Der Entwicklungsprozess endet, wenn vorher definierte Zielwerte für die Fitness erreicht sind.

So wie heute bereits selbstverständlich Formen vom Computer generiert werden, ist es absehbar, dass die einstige Utopie automatisch generierter und optimierter Tragkonstruktionen bald Wirklichkeit wird.

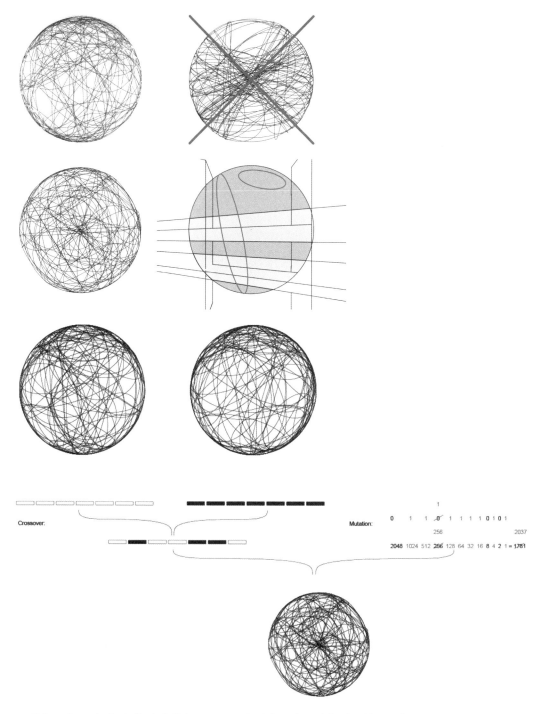

Sphere, Deutsche Bank, Mario Bellini, structure evolved through predefined architectural
and structural fitness criteria, 2009–11

Miscellanea of Ingenious Architecture in the Soviet Avant-Garde

Frank Rolf Werner

Miszellen zu ingeniösen Architekturen zuzeiten der sowjetischen Avantgarde

Frank Rolf Werner

"Not the old, not the new, but the necessary"
V. Tatlin, Moscow 1920

The times in which knowledge about Russian revolutionary art and architecture was some sort of tabula rasa and suppressed by political forces in the Soviet Union are long past. Even before the fall of the system, scholars began focussing on artifacts created by A.V. Lunacharsky's and A. Bogdanov's "Proletkult" during the young nation's economically and politically severe post-revolutionary years. Here has research focussed mainly on the great number of temporary Agitprop installations by the so-called "Street Art,"[1] but also on post-revolutionary art debates,[2] and, of course, artistic innovations like Malevich's suprematist paintings, El Lissitzky's "Proun," and many other icons of revolutionary art.[3]

»Nicht das Alte, nicht das Neue, aber das Notwendige«
W. Tatlin, Moskau 1920

Die Zeiten, in denen das Wissen um die russische Revolutionskunst und -architektur eine Art von »tabula rasa« verkörperte, ja von den politischen Verhältnissen in der Sowjetunion regelrecht unterdrückt wurde, sind lange vorbei. Dabei hatte sich das wissenschaftliche Interesse schon vor dem Zusammenbruch der Sowjetunion verstärkt auf jene Artefakte konzentriert, welche in den nachrevolutionären, wirtschaftlich und politisch anfänglich sehr schweren Jahren im Rahmen des von A.W. Lunatscharski und A. Bogdanov initi-ierten »Proletkults« entstanden waren. Dabei handelte es sich um den großen Kom-plex temporärer Agitprop-Installationen

At the beginning of the 1970s, almost forty years after the end of revolutionary Russian architecture, Kyrill N. Afanasjev produced the first very short summary of post-revolutionary building projects. The first comprehensive academic study, by Selim O. Khan-Magomedov, did not appear until 1983.[4] It not only highlighted the importance of the Vkhutemas technical school, often called the "Russian Bauhaus," but also the diversity of various, in part fiercely competing, groups of architects. Architect unions like SCHIWSKULPTARCH, INKhUK, ASNOVA, MAO, OSA, ARU, and WOPRA had to perform in a theoretical and practical balancing act between academic, traditionally oriented and avant-garde thinking and design positions. Konstantin Melnikov's dynamic pavilion for the Exposition Internationale des Arts Décoratifs et Industriels Modernes in Paris in 1925 was seen worldwide as the figurehead of the new avant-garde spirit of optimism in Russia. In reality, though, it could not hide the fact that many diverging trends existed in revolutionary architecture.

No other institution manifested these trends as clearly as the WChUTEMAS, which stood far too long in the shadow of the much smaller Bauhaus. Not until 1990 was it possible to publish a two-volume paper, which dealt solely with the WChUTEMAS[5] as well as the original programmatic, theoretical, and artistic positions of its lecturers. A year later, the Kunsthalle Tübingen, in cooperation with the Moscow Museum of Architecture, held the first comprehensive exhibition in Germany, which focussed exclusively on the history, rise, and decline of the Russian Soviet avant-garde between 1900

der sogenannten »Street Art«,[1] aber auch um die nachrevolutionären Kunstdebatten[2] und natürlich die künstlerischen Neuerungen, wie etwa Malewitschs suprematistische Malereien. El Lissitzkys »Proune« und viele andere Ikonen der Revolutionskunst.[3]

Nachdem Kyrill N. Afanasjew zu Anfang der 1970er Jahren, also fast vierzig Jahre nach Ende der Russischen Revolutionsarchitektur, eine erste, wenngleich noch sehr schmale Übersicht über das nachrevolutionäre Baugeschehen geliefert hatte, legte Selim O. Chan-Magomedow 1983 die bis dahin umfassendste und wissenschaftlich fundierteste Studie zur russischen Revolutionsarchitektur vor.[4] In ihr wurde nicht nur die Bedeutung der immer wieder als »russisches Bauhaus« titulierten Ausbildungsstätte WChUTEMAS herausgestellt sondern auch die Vielgestaltigkeit der unterschiedlichen, teilweise heftig miteinander rivalisierenden Architektengruppen dargestellt. Architektenverbände wie SCHIWSKULPTARCH, INChUK, ASNOWA, MAO, OSA, ARU oder WOPRA hatten nämlich in ihren eigenen Reihen den theoretischen wie praktischen Spagat zwischen akademischen, traditionell orientierten und avantgardistischen Denk- und Entwurfspositionen zu bewältigen. Konstantin Melnikovs dynamischer Pavillon auf der Pariser Exposition Internationale des Arts Décoratifs et Industriels Modernes des Jahre 1925 galt zwar weltweit als das Aushängeschild der neuen avantgardistischen Aufbruchstimmung in Russland. Realiter vermochte er aber kaum über die divergierenden Strömungen innerhalb der Revolutionsarchitektur hinweg zu täuschen.

Shukhov Tower, 1922, Alexander Rodchenko © VBK, Wien 2011

and 1937. The accompanying illustrated books contain many essays that are still deemed key texts today and shed light on the status of research at the end of the twentieth century.[6]

What is striking about current scholarly work is the fact that with the exception of drawn constructive visions or utopias, there is almost no information about the ingenious achievements of Soviet revolutionary architects. This is astonishing if we consider that Russia boasted the very talented engineer V.G. Shukhov, whose career began during the times of the Czar.

In his early years, Shukhov had already developed highly advanced bearing structures for bridges, industrial buildings, train stations, passages, and other facilities. And he was able to build a wide array of "hyperbolic grid towers"[7] topped with water containers all over Russia. But worldwide renown for Shukhov only came in 1922 when he built the tower for the Shabolovka radio station in Moscow. The height of the tower, which was originally intended to be 350 meters and thus would have dwarfed the Eiffel Tower, was reduced to 150 meters due to a lack of building material. The impressive construction, which still stands today, consists of six hyperbolic frame segments, one on top of the other, which narrow towards the final antenna. For many years, the radio tower was the highest building in the country. Comparisons to the Eiffel Tower were more than flattering, as Shukhov's tower was seen as the far more advanced, avant-garde lightweight construction. Together with Tatlin's unrealized *Monument to the Third International*, it became iconic of a young Soviet Union reaching for the skies.

An keiner anderen Institution traten diese Strömungen so deutlich zutage wie an der WChUTEMAS, die viel zu lange im Schatten des erheblich kleineren Bauhauses stand. Erst 1990 war es möglich, eine zweibändige Studie zu publizieren, die sich ausschließlich der WChUTEMAS widmete[5] und die programmatischen, theoretischen wie künstlerischen Ausgangspositionen der dort Lehrenden eingehend analysierte. Ein Jahr später veranstaltete dann die Kunsthalle Tübingen in Kooperation mit dem Moskauer Architekturmuseum die erste umfassende Ausstellung in Deutschland, die sich ausschließlich auf die Vorgeschichte, die Blütezeit und den Untergang der russisch-sowjetischen Architektur-avantgarde im Zeitraum von 1900 bis 1937 fokussierte. Die begleitenden Katalogbände enthalten neben dem Katalogteil zahlreiche Aufsätze, die bis heute als Schlüsseltexte gelten und Aufschluss geben über den Forschungsstand des ausgehenden 20. Jahrhunderts.[6]

Was bei den inzwischen vorliegenden wissenschaftlichen Arbeiten auffällt, ist der Umstand, dass mit Ausnahme gezeichneter konstruktiver Visionen oder Utopien von ingeniösen Leistungen der sowjetischen Revolutionsarchitektur in nahezu allen Fällen vergleichsweise wenig die Rede ist. Das ist erstaunlich, wenn man den Umstand bedenkt, dass Russland etwa mit W. G. Šuchov über einen außerordentlich begabten Ingenieur verfügte, dessen Karriere bereits in der Zarenzeit begonnen hatte. In seinen frühen Jahren entwickelte Šuchov bereits sehr fortschrittliche Tragwerke für Brücken, Industriebauten, Bahnhöfe, Passagen und andere Einrichtungen. Und er konnte russlandweit eine große Anzahl von

Russian revolutionary architecture produced many similarly ambitious, but often unrealized and sometimes unrealizable projects. Be it Chernikhov's machine forms and fantasies, Lissitzky's Lenin Tribune (an adapted student project) or his Cloud Iron, or the designs of the Wesnin brothers for the "Leningradskaya Pravda" and the Palace of Work, the constructions always stood in the limelight not so much for their inherent qualities, but due to their constructivist expression. Constructivism was taught together with the only slightly different rationalism in many post-revolutionary schools in Leningrad and Moscow. This was also true for the WChUTEMAS, whose intellectual leader was the architect Nikolai Alexandrovich Ladovsky, who also taught at other schools. He emphasized that spatial thinking had to take priority over the consideration of artistic aspects and construction. At the WChUTEMAS, he was founder of the United Workshops (Obmas), which were only active for three years, but these years are among the most important in the history of modern Soviet architecture. According to Khan-Magomedov, these workshops were the real creative laboratories in which new architecture was born in Soviet Russia. "Ladovsky proposed a teaching method that would develop from the abstract to the concrete. He thought that students' heads should not be filled with facts and architectural details during the first phase of their studies. He started out rather by developing his students' imagination and way of thinking and forced them to adopt logical and artistic models. This method produced results: the students soon developed creative thinking. Although they did not

»hyperbolischen Gittertürmen«[7] bauen, die von Wasserbehältern bekrönt wurden. Weltweite Anerkennung erreichte Šuchov jedoch erst mit seinem 1922 in Betrieb genommenen Sendeturm für die Moskauer Radiostation Sabolovka. Die Turmhöhe, die ursprünglich auf 350 Metern angelegt war, womit der Sendeturm höher als der Pariser Eiffelturm gewesen wäre, wurde aus Materialmangel auf 150 Meter beschränkt. Die eindrucksvolle, noch existierende Konstruktion besteht aus sechs übereinander gestellten, hyperbolischen Stabwerksegmenten, die sich zur abschließenden Antenne hin kontinuierlich verjüngen. Viele Jahre lang war der Sendeturm das höchste Bauwerk des Landes. Der Vergleich mit dem Eifelturm fiel mehr als schmeichelhaft aus, galt Šuchovs Turm doch als sehr viel fortschrittlichere, avantgardistische Leichtbaukonstruktion. Diese wurde zusammen mit Tatlins nicht ausgeführtem Turmmonument für die III. Internationale zum Aushängeschild einer jungen, himmelwärts stürmenden Sowjetunion.

Ähnlich kühne, aber nicht ausgeführte, ja mitunter gar nicht ausführbare Projekte hat die russische Revolutionsarchitektur in großer Zahl hervorgebracht. Ganz gleich ob es sich dabei um Tschernichovs Maschinenanalogien und Phantasien, Lissitzkys Lenin-Tribüne (Anm.: eine adaptierte Studentenarbeit), Lissitzkys Wolkenbügel oder die Entwürfe bzw. Wettbewerbsentwürfe der Gebrüder Wesnin für die »Leningradskaja Prawda« und den Palast der Arbeit handelte, stets standen konstruierte Konstruktionen weniger um ihrer selbst willen im Vordergrund als vielmehr ihres konstruktivistischen Ausdrucks zuliebe. Gelehrt wurde dieser

know many things yet, they created inventive designs. Ladovsky unleashed the students' creative reserves and taught them a method of creative thinking instead of a repertoire of indivi-dual design processes."[8] Ladovsky's lessons ranged from questions of the geometrical and physicalmechanical characteristics of forms to the expression of mass and weight and, finally, to definitions of construction and space. The last step included the ultimate definition of dynamics, rhythm and proportionality on the plane as well as on the vertical axis.

Many of WChUTEMAS' student research projects created under the tutelage of Ladovsky, such as S. Lapatin's work dealing with the topic of the "lever" or the work of I.N. Varencov dealing with the subject of the "beam," attest to an extraordinarily vital, ingenious force.[9] Many other student projects are documented. One work seemed so important to El Lissitzky that he included it under the title "Studio N. Ladovsky, 1922" in his famous 1930 anthology on Soviet architecture.[10] The project shows a high, protruding wall of rock. From this wall of rock, a dynamically skewed and seemingly extremely unstable steel construction protrudes even further. It is connected to the wall only at certain intervals and contains a restaurant with a view and some additional staged rooms. The "flying" levels of the facility can be reached via a cable car. The exercise resulted in a picture, which deconstructs the real construction in favor of an almost surreal expression of dynamism and floating. The anthology features another work, no less spectacular but slightly more realistic, by M. Korschev, another of Ladovsky's former pupils. It is a

Konstruktivismus zusammen mit dem sich nur in Nuancen unterscheidenden, wahlverwandten Rationalismus an vielen nachrevolutionären Ausbildungsstätten in Leningrad und Moskau. So auch an der Moskauer WChUTEMAS. Geistiger Führer war dort der auch an anderen Schulen tätige Architekt Nikolaj Aleksandrovic Ladowski. Er betonte, dass das räumliche Denken Priorität genießen müsse gegenüber dem Umgang mit künstlerischen Aspekten und der Konstruktion. An der WChUTEMAS war Ladowski Gründer der »Vereinigten Werkstatt« (Obmas). Nur drei Jahre lang war Letztere aktiv (1920–1923) und dennoch zählen diese Jahre zu den wichtigsten in der Geschichte der modernen sowjetischen Architektur. Denn laut Chan-Magomedow war diese Werkstatt das eigentliche schöpferische Laboratorium, in dem die neue Architektur in Sowjetrussland tatsächlich geboren wurde. »Ladowski schlug eine Unterrichtsmethode vor, die vom Abstrakten zum Konkreten führte. Er war der Meinung, dass es in der ersten Zeit des Studiums nicht darauf ankomme, die Studenten mit Fakten und architektonischen Details zu spicken. Er begann vielmehr mit den Methoden, entwickelte bei den Studenten eine Methode des Denkens und der Vorstellung und zwang sie dazu, sich logische und gestalterische Modelle anzueignen. Diese Methode zeigte ihre Resultate: Bei den Studenten entwickelte sich schnell das schöpferische Denken. Obgleich sie vieles noch nicht wussten, schufen sie dennoch originelle Entwürfe. Ladowski setzte die schöpferischen Reserven der Studenten frei und vermittelte ihnen eine Methode schöpferischen Denkens an Stelle eines Repertoires von einzelnen Entwurfsverfahren.«[8] Nach

Restaurant and landing over a slope, Studio N. Ladovsky (WChUTEMAS), 1922; Drawing by Florian Unterberger, 2012

cross-section "of the tribunes for the stadium in Moscow 1926," which shows a statically breathtaking equilibristic piece of art. It is remotely reminiscent of a cross-section made by Ladovsky himself in 1920 for a commune dwelling. Lissitzky says of Korschev's project, "Most characteristic and striking about this design is the formation of the tribune, which is a massive cantilevered reinforced concrete and steel lattice structure. Situated at the bottom is the motor racing circuit, which is followed by a line of seats, roofed by a protruding lane for the motorcycle and cycle races. Above that, additional seats rise up to the buckling of the protruding support, on which five rows of closed cabins are hung ... here, constructive and formative elements are consciously combined."[11] What an understatement, considering that the cross-section does not only paint a constructive and dynamic picture but also a highly political one, showing all watching and working people as equals!

Another work that made it into Lissitzky's anthology is one of the most famous diploma projects of Soviet revolutionary architecture. The work included though is not, as one would assume, Georgy Krutikov's *Flying City* (1928) but Ivan Leonidov's project, *Lenin Institute* (1927). Leonidov was not a Ladovsky pupil, but a graduate of Alexander Vesnin. His diploma project became one of the best-known ones of the Russian avant-garde soon after its publication and even brought him a Chair at the WChUTEMAS. The design for the Lenin Institute was originally conceived as a state library consisting of a lecture hall, five reading rooms, a book depot on ropes and an aerial railway station connecting the ensemble with the city center. Andrei Gozak

Festlegung der geometrischen und physikalisch-mechanischen Eigenschaften der Form leiteten Ladowskis Übungen zur Festlegung des Ausdrucks von Masse und Gewicht und weiter zur Festlegung der Konstruktion und des Raums an. Der letzte Übungsschritt umfasste schließlich die endgültige Definition von Dynamik, Rhythmus und Proportionalität in der Fläche sowie in der Vertikalen.

Zahlreiche der an der WChUTEMAS unter Ladowskis Anleitung entstandenen Studienarbeiten bezeugen eine ungemein vitale, ingeniöse Kraft. So zum Beispiel die Arbeit des Studenten S. Lapatin zum Thema »Hebel« oder die des Studenten I.N. Varencov zum Thema »Träger«.[9] Viele andere Studienprojekte sind dokumentiert. Eine weitere Arbeit erschien El Lissitzky immerhin so bedeutend, dass er sie betitelt mit »Atelier N. Ladowski 1922« in seine berühmte Anthologie zur neuen sowjetischen Architektur aus dem Jahre 1930 aufnahm.[10] Das Projekt zeigt uns eine hohe, weit überkragende Felswand. An diese schiefe Felswand und mit ihr nur noch punktuell verbunden, erkennt man eine dynamisch schräge, noch weiter auskragende und extrem instabil wirkende Stahlkonstruktion geheftet, die ein Aussichtsrestaurant nebst weiteren, darunter gestaffelten Räumen aufnimmt. Erschlossen werden die »fliegenden« Ebenen der Gesamtanlage durch eine Schrägseilbahn. Bei dieser Übung ist ein Bild entstanden, welches die reale Konstruktion dekonstruiert zugunsten eines fast schon surreal anmutenden Ausdrucks von Dynamik und Schwebeleichtigkeit. Lissitzky präsentiert in seiner Anthologie noch eine weitere, nicht minder spektakuläre, allerdings etwas handfestere

and Andrei Leonidov depicted the project in its original form in detail and with original Russian texts.[12]

It is astonishing even today to see what a delicate balance the young Leonidov struck between the disparate bodies of his decidedly structural design, including the auditorium's seemingly totally unstable supported glass sphere. Frampton called the design a brilliant "synthesis between the tectonic syntax of constructivism and floating, dematerialised forms, inspired by the visionary iconography of Kazimir Malevich suprematism."[13] At a time when constructivism was in danger of being degraded to a simple stylistic application, Leonidov succeeded in creating a completely "renewed coherence but, above all, a fundamentally renewed comprehension of form and construction."[14]

Leonidov's design comprised a high rise for the storage of books, a low building for reading and work rooms, a "floating" globular auditorium situated on top of a funnel shaped framework, which was also to function as a planetarium, and an aerial railway connecting the city. These elements were all arranged around a coordinate plane. Situated in front of it is a circular glass pavilion, marking the shifted transversal axis, above which the auditorium's glass sphere seems to float. This arrangement cannot be implemented, of course, without special technical precautions. So, according to Adolf Max Vogt, the high rise and the sphere were braced with wire rope, which is normally only used for antenna masts. "These wirings are optically important so that the whole facility gets a clear *constructive* factor. The *functional* factor is to enable a clear division of

Arbeit. Sie stammt von M. Korschew, einem ehemaligen Ladowski-Schüler, und zeigt den Querschnitt »durch die Tribünen für das Stadion in Moskau 1926«. Der Schnitt führt uns ein statisch atemberaubendes equilibristisches Kunststück vor Augen. Und er erinnert entfernt an einen Schnitt, den Ladowski 1920 selbst für das Projekt eines Kommunewohnhauses angefertigt hatte. Lissitzky merkt zu Korschews Projekt an: »Das charakteristischste und schlagendste an diesem Entwurf ist die Ausbildung der Tribüne. Es ist eine mächtige konsolartige Eisenbeton- und Eisenfachwerkkonstruktion. Ganz unten ist das Autodrom, dann kommen eine Reihe Plätze, die von einem auskragenden Weg für das Motorrad- und Radrennen überdacht sind. Darüber steigen weitere Plätze bis zur Knickung zu der wieder nah vorne ragenden Konsole, an der fünf Reihen geschlossene Kabinen aufgehängt sind ... Hier sind konstruktive und gestaltende Elemente bewusst vereinigt.«[11] Was für ein Understatement, verkörpert der Schnitt durch diese Tribüne doch in Wahrheit ein zwar konstruktiv dynamisch angelegtes, letztlich aber zutiefst politisch gemeintes Bild von der unterschieds- oder ranglosen Gleichheit zuschauender werktätiger Menschen.

Ebenfalls in Lissitzkys Anthologie aufgenommen wurde eine der berühmtesten Diplomarbeiten der sowjetischen Revolutionsarchitektur. Gemeint ist nicht die der »fliegenden Stadt der Zukunft« (1928) von Georgii Kruitikov, sondern das Projekt »Lenin Institut« (1927) von Ivan Leonidov. Dieser war kein Schüler von Ladovskiy sondern ein Absolvent Alexander Wesnins. Leonidovs Diplomarbeit aus dem Jahre 1927 avancierte bereits kurz nach ihrer

operations: reading, the storing of books, and the gathering for scientific exchange are all done in three different and distinctly shaped buildings. Thus work themes are included in Leonidov's concept, although the concept at first glance only seems to be pure geometry ... coordinate plane and a sphere. This highest demand on stereometrical clearance was used for a certain purpose: Library—the development of education for the working classes—worker culture. This purpose is found in two basic characteristics of astronomy: the sphere as the basic astronomic element and the coordinate plane as the astronomic organising principle."[15]

The basic astronomic element and the astronomic organising principle are two aspects alluded to by A.M. Vogt, which—at least subliminally—were integrated into Vladimir Tatlin's unrealized *Monument to the Third International* from the years 1919 to 1920. This monument is a deeply symbolic piece of art and, at the same time, an ingenious functional building. Tatlin, who was called an "artist of material culture" by L.A. Shadowa,[16] spoke about not having done the old or the new, but the necessary. Nikolai Nikolayevich Punin, Tatlin's earliest biographer, was the first to talk about the importance of the helix. "The use and organisation of the helix in its modern form is in itself already an enrichment of composition. Just as the proportion of parts was expressed best by the triangle during the Renaissance, the spirit of our times is best expressed through the helix. The correlation of gravity and pier is the purest (classical) form of statics; the classical form of dynamics is the helix. Societies of class antagonism fought for the possession of land, their direction of movement is horizontal; the

Fertigstellung zu einem der bekanntesten Projekte der russischen Avantgarde und brachte ihm umgehend sogar eine Professur an der WChUTEMAS ein. Der Entwurf für das Lenin-Institut war eigentlich die Konzeption einer Staatsbibliothek, bestehend aus einem Vortragssaal, fünf Lesesälen, einem an Seilen aufgehängten Büchermagazin und einer Hochbahnhaltestelle, die das Ensemble mit dem Stadtzentrum verbinden sollte. Andrei Gozak und Andrei Leonidov haben das Projekt in seiner ursprünglichen Fassung, versehen mit den russischen Originaltexten, ausführlich dargestellt.[12] Frappierend wirkt noch heute, mit welch schlafwandlerischer Sicherheit der junge Leonidov die disparaten Einzelkörper seines dezidiert konstruktiv angelegten Entwurfs, darunter vor allem die scheinbar völlig instabil aufgeständerte Glaskugel des Auditoriums, gegeneinander ausponderiert hat. Damit gelang dem Entwurf nach Frampton eine brillante »Synthese zwischen der tektonischen Syntax des Konstruktivismus und schwebenden, entmaterialisierten Formen, die von der visionären Ikonografie des Suprematismus von Kasimir Malewitsch inspiriert waren.«[13] In einer Zeit, in welcher der Konstruktivismus Gefahr lief, zu einer rein stilistischen Applikation zu verkommen, gelang Leonidov mithin eine gänzlich »erneuerte Kohärenz, vor allem aber ein grundlegend erneuertes Verständnis von Form und Konstruktion«.[14]

Leonidov gliederte seinen Entwurf in ein Hochhaus für die Bücheraufbewahrung, einen Flachbau für die Lese- und Arbeitsräume, ein auf einem trichterförmigen Stabwerk »schwebenden« kugelförmigen Auditorium, welches laut Erläuterungstext aus als Planetarium fungieren sollte, und eine Hochbahnstation für die Verbindung

Reconstruction of Ivan Leonidow's Lenin-Institute (1927) 1992/93

Unbuildable Tatlin?!

helix is the direction of the movement of the freed human being. The helix is the ideal expression of liberation; by planting its foot on the ground, it moves and thus becomes the symbol of liberation from all animalistic, earthly, and submissive interests."[17]

We have come full circle in this short excursus, which attempts to show how deeply Tatlin's unique tower monument was embedded in avant-garde achievements of engineering on the one hand and the artistic conquest of new territories on the other hand. That Tatlin had thus opened the proverbial Pandora's Box is evident in the numerous ingenious architectural projections of younger and the youngest of architects during the following years. But nobody, with the exception perhaps of Leonidov, came near Tatlin's powerfully charged picture in the subsequent decade. After that, the heroic phase of Soviet constructivism, which operated in society by creating innovative design, had almost elapsed again. What remains for us are paper documents and models; what is left is the adventure of ideas. The few constructions that could be built during those times are now in danger of being destroyed forever due to insufficient building maintenance.

1   Vladimir Tolstoy, Irina Bibikova, Catherine Cooke (eds), *Street Art of the Revolution, Festivals and Celebrations in Russia 1918–33*, Moscow, 1984, London, 1990.
2   Hubertus Gaßner and Eckhart Gillen (eds), *Zwischen Revolutionskunst und Sozialistischem Realismus, Dokumente und Kommentare, Kunstdebatten in der Sowjetunion von 1917 bis 1934*, Cologne, 1979; John E. Bowlt (ed.), *Russian Art of the Avantgarde, Theory and Criticism*, London, 1976 (2nd edn 1988, 3rd edn 1990).
3   Larissa A. Shadowa, *Suche und Experiment, Russische und Sowjetische Kunst 1910 bis 1930*, Dresden, 1978.

zur Stadt. Diese Bauteile ordnete er um ein Achsenkreuz an. Diesem vorgelagert ist ein kreisförmiger Glaspavillon, der die verschobene Querachse markiert, über der die gläserne Kugel des Auditoriums zu schweben scheint. Dieses Arrangement ist freilich nicht möglich ohne besondere Vorkehrungen technischer Art. So werden Hochhaus und Kugel nach Adolf Max Vogt mit Drahtseilen so verspannt und fixiert, wie man ansonsten nur Antennenmasten fixiert. »Diese Verspannungen sind optisch so wichtig, dass die Anlage einen deutlichen konstruktiven Faktor bekommt. Der funktionelle Faktor liegt in der klaren Aufteilung der Tätigkeiten: Das Lesen, das Aufbewahren der Bücher und das Versammeln zum wissenschaftlichen Austausch vollziehen sich in drei verschiedenen, auch verschieden geformten Gebäuden. Arbeitsmotive sind also bei Leonidov durchaus mit im Konzept, wiewohl das Konzept zunächst nur reine Geometrie, und nur das, zu sein scheint ... Achsenkreuz und Kugel. Dieser höchste Anspruch an stereometrische Klärung wurde für einen bestimmten Zeck eingesetzt: Bibliothek – Erarbeitung einer Bildung der Arbeiterklasse – Arbeiterkultur. Dieser Zweck findet seine Gestalt in den zwei Grundformen der Astronomie: Der Kugel als dem astronomischen Elementarkörper, dem Koordinatenkreuz als dem astronomischen Ordnungsprinzip.«[15]

Mit dem astronomischen Elementarkörper und dem astronomischen Ordnungsprinzip hat A. M. Vogt zwei wesentliche Aspekte angesprochen, die – zumindest unterschwellig – auch in Wladimir Tatlins unausgeführtes Monument für die III. Internationale aus den Jahren 1919 bis 1920 eingeflossen sind. Dieses Monument ist

4   Kyrill N. Afanasjew, *Ideen-Projekte-Bauten,
    Sowjetische Architektur 1917–32*, Selim O. Khan-
    Magomedow, *Pioniere der sowjetischen Architektur*,
    Vienna and Berlin, 1983.

5   Selim O. Khan-Magomedow, *Vhutemas: Kunst
    Fotografie Design Architektur, Moskau 1920–30*,
    Paris, 1990.

6   Scusev-Architekturmuseum Moskau, Institut für
    Auslandsbeziehungen Stuttgart, Kunsthalle
    Tübingen (eds), *Avantgarde I 1900–1923, Russisch-
    sowjetische Architektur, Avantgarde II 1924–1937,
    Sowjetische Architektur*, Stuttgart, 1991.

7   Cf. Irina A. Petropavlovskaja, "Hyperbolische
    Gittertürme" in V.G. Shukhov (ed.), *Institut für
    Auslandsbeziehungen Stuttgart, Scusev-
    Architekturmuseum Moskau, Institut für leichte
    Flächentragwerke der Universität Stuttgart Teilprojekt
    C3 "Geschichte des Konstruierens" des
    Sonderforschungsbereichs 230, 1853–1939*,
    Stuttgart, 1990, pp.78–79.

8   Selim O. Khan-Magomedow, "Bedingungen und
    Besonderheiten in der Entstehung der Avantgarde
    in der sowjetischen Architektur", in Kunsthalle
    Tübingen (1991), p.27.

9   Selim O. Khan-Magomedow, 1991, pp.88–89.

10 El Lissitzky, *Russland, Neues Bauen in der Welt, Bd.
    1*, Vienna, 1930, p.48.

11 Lissitzky 1930, p.23.

12 Andrei Gozak and Andrei Leonidov, *Ivan Leonidov:
    The Complete Works*, London, 1988, pp.42ff.

13 Kenneth Frampton, "Leonidov", in V.M.
    Lampugnani (ed.), *Hatje Lexikon der Architektur des
    20. Jahrhunderts*, Ostfildern-Ruit, 1998, p.223.

14 Selim O. Khan-Magomedow, "I.L. Leonidov
    1902–1959", in O.A. Shvidkovsky, *Building in the
    USSR 1917–1932*, London, 1971, p.124.

15 Adolf Max Vogt, *Russische und Französische
    Revolutionsarchitektur 1789–1917*, Cologne 1974,
    pp.205–206.

16 Larissa Alexejewena Shadowa (ed.), *Tatlin*,
    Weingarten 1987, p.88.

17 N. Punin, *Das Denkmal der III. Internationale, Ein
    Projekt des Künstlers W.J. Tatlin*, Petrograd 1920,
    cited in Shadowa 1987, p.413; cf. also W.J. Tatlin,
    Gegen den Kubismus, Petrograd 1921, pp.21–22.

nämlich gleichermaßen symbolträchtiges Kunstwerk wie ingeniöser Zweckbau. Tatlin, den L. A. Shadowa als »Künstler der materiellen Kultur« bezeichnet hat,[16] sprach davon, nicht das Alte, nicht das Neue, aber das Notwendige getan zu haben. Und Nikolai Nikolajewisch Punin, Tatlins frühester Biograf, sprach zum ersten Mal von der Bedeutung der Spirale. »Die Verwendung und Organisation der Spirale in der modernen Form ist schon an sich eine Bereicherung der Komposition. Ähnlich wie in der Renaissance die Proportion der Teile am besten durch das Dreieck ausgedrückt wurde, kommt der Geist unserer Zeit am besten durch die Spirale zum Ausdruck. Die Wechselwirkung von Schwerkraft und Stützpfeiler ist die reinste (klassische) Form der Statik; die klassische Form der Dynamik ist die Spirale. Die Gesellschaftsformen der Klassengegensätze kämpften um den Besitz von Grund und Boden, ihre Bewegungslinie ist horizontal; die Spirale ist die Bewegungslinie des befreiten Menschen. Die Spirale ist der ideale Ausdruck der Befreiung; indem sich ihr Fuß in die Erde stemmt, bewegt sich dieselbe und wird gleichsam zum Symbol für die Befreiung von allen tierischen, irdischen und unterwürfigen Interessen.«[17]

Damit schließt sich der Zirkelschlag eines kurzen Exkurses, dessen Absicht es war, aufzuzeigen, wie sehr Tatlins einzigartiges Turmmonument eingebettet war in avantgardistische Ingenieurleistungen einerseits und künstlerisches Eroberungen neuer Territorien andererseits. Damit hatte Tatlin die sprichwörtliche Büchse der Pandora geöffnet, was uns die zahllosen ingeniösen Architekturprojektionen jüngerer und jüngster Architekten in den Folgejahren

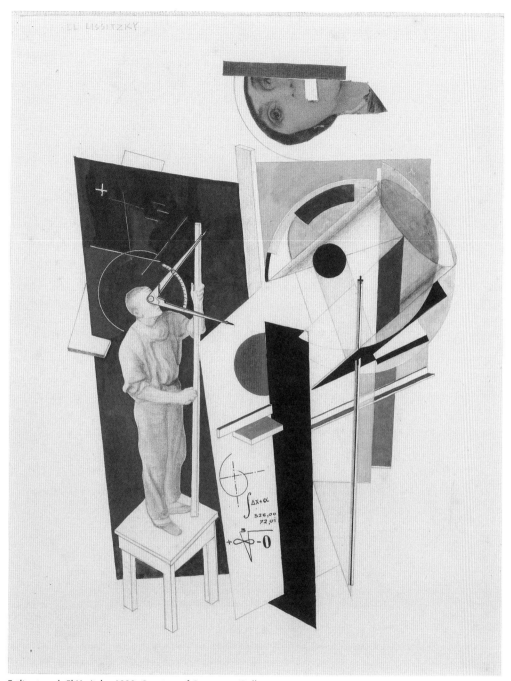

Tatlin at work, El Lissitzky, 1922. Courtesy of Grosvenor Gallery

Tatlin's Tower

deutlich bewiesen haben. Aber niemand, vielleicht niemand außer Leonidov, dürfte Tatlins kraftvoll aufgeladenem Bild im darauf folgenden Jahrzehnt auch nur nahe gekommen sein. Und dann war die heroische Phase eines gesellschaftlich mit innovativen Bildern operierenden sowjetischen Konstruktivismus auch schon fast wieder am Ende. Geblieben sind uns aber wenigstens papierne Dokumente und Modelle, geblieben ist uns das Abenteuer der Ideen. Denn das Wenige, was in dieser Zeit gebaut werden konnte, ist aufgrund mangelhafter Bauunterhaltung heute vielfach von Zerfall bedroht.

1   Vladimir Tolstoy, Irina Bibikova, Catherine Cooke (Hrsg.), *Street Art of the Revolution, Festivals and Celebrations in Russia 1918–33*, Moskau 1984, London 1990.
2   Hubertus Gaßner, Eckhart Gillen (Hrsg.), *Zwischen Revolutionskunst und Sozialistischem Realismus, Dokumente und Kommentare, Kunstdebatten in der Sowjetunion von 1917 bis 1934*, Köln 1979; John, E. Bowlt (Hrsg.), *Russian Art of the Avantgarde, Theory and Criticism*, London 1976 (2nd 1988, 3rd 1990).
3   Larissa A. Shadowa, *Suche und Experiment, Russische und sowjetische Kunst 1910 bis 1930*, Dresden 1978.
4   Kyrill N. Afanasjew, *Ideen-Projekte-Bauten, Sowjetische Architektur 1917/32*; Selim O. Chan-Magomedow, *Pioniere der sowjetischen Architektur*, Wien und Berlin 1983.
5   Selim O. Chan-Magemodow, *VHUTEMAS, Kunst Fotografie Design Architektur, Moskau 1920–30*, Paris 1990.
6   Scusev-Architekturmuseum Moskau, Institut für Auslandsbeziehungen Stuttgart, Kunsthalle Tübingen (Hrsg.), *Avantgarde I 1900–1923, Russisch-sowjetische Architektur, Avantgarde II 1924–1937, Sowjetische Architektur*, Stuttgart 1991.
7   vergl. hierzu: Irina A. Petropavlovskaja, »Hyperbolische Gittertürme«, in: *Institut für Auslandsbeziehungen Stuttgart, Scusev-Architekturmuseum Moskau, Institut für leichte Flächentragwerke der Universität Stuttgart Teilprojekt C3 »Geschichte des Konstruierens« des Sonderforschungsbereichs 230* (Hrsg.), W. G. Šuchov 1853–1939, Stuttgart 1990, S. 78 f.
8   Selim O. Chan-Magomedow, »Bedingungen und Besonderheiten in der Entstehung der Avantgarde in der sowjetischen Architektur«, in: Kunsthalle Tübingen (Hrsg.), s. Anm. 6, *Avantgarde I 1900–1923*, S. 27.
9   ebenda, S. 88 und 89.
10 El Lissitzky, *Russland, Neues Bauen in der Welt*, Bd. 1, Wien 1930, S. 48.
11 ebenda. S. 23.
12 Andrei Gozak & Andrei Leonidov, *Ivan Leonidov, The Complete Works*, London 1988, S. 42 ff.
13 Kenneth Frampton, »Leonidov«, in: *Hatje Lexikon der Architektur des 20. Jahrhunderts*, V.M. Lampugnani (Hrsg.), Ostfildern-Ruit 1998, S. 223.
14 Selim O. Chan-Magemedov, *I.L. Leonidov 1902–1959*, in: O.A. Shvidkovsky, *Building in the USSR 1917–1932*, London 1971, S. 124.
15 Adolf Max Vogt, *Russische und Französische Revolutionsarchitektur 1789–1917*, Köln 1974, S. 205 f.
16 Larissa Alexejewena Shadowa (Hrsg.), *Tatlin*, Weingarten 1987, S. 88.
17 N. Punin, *Das Denkmal der III. Internationale, Ein Projekt des Künstlers W.J. Tatlin*, Petrograd 1920, zit. in: L.A. Shadowa (Hrsg.), s. Anm. 16, S. 413; vergl. hierzu auch: Tatlin, *Gegen den Kubismus*, Petrograd 1921, S. 21 f.

Specific section

Spezieller Teil

The Work Awaiting Us

V. Y. Tatlin
T. Shapiro
I. Meyerzon
P. Vinogradov

Die Arbeit, die uns erwartet

W. J. Tatlin
T. Schapiro
I. Meierson
P. Winogradow

The foundation on which our artistic work—our trade—rested was not homogeneous any more and every connection between painting, sculpting, and architecture had been lost. The result was individualism, which gave rise to an expression of simple personal habits and tastes, with artists often using materials in a grotesque way in relation to one or another field of fine arts. At best, artists decorated the walls of private houses—individual nests—and left us with a number of "Jaroslaw train stations" and a variety of forms that are now ridiculous.

What happened socially in 1917 had already been implemented in our fine arts in 1914 when we made "material, volume, and construction" the foundation of our work. We do not rely on our eyes any more and we bring our sensations under control. In 1915, an exhibition in

Das Fundament, auf dem unser bildnerisches Werk – unser Handwerk – ruhte, war nicht homogen und jeder Zusammenhang zwischen Malerei, Bildhauerei und Architektur war verloren gegangen. Die Folge davon war Individualismus, d.h. Ausdruck rein persönlicher Gewohnheiten und Geschmacksinteressen, wobei die Künstler in Bezug auf das eine oder andere Gebiet der bildenden Kunst in oft entstellender Weise mit dem Material umgegangen sind. Im besten Falle schmückten die Künstler die Wände von Privathäusern – individuelle Nester – und hinterließen uns eine Reihe von »Jaroslaw-Bahnhöfen« und ein Varieté von jetzt lächerlichen Formen.

Was 1917 sich in sozialer Hinsicht ereignete, war schon 1914 innerhalb unserer bildenden Kunst verwirklicht, als wir »Material, Volumen und Konstruktion« zum Fundament unserer Arbeit machten. Wir

Vladimir Tatlin and his assistants I.A. Meerzon and T.M. Shapiro constructing the first model for the *Monument to the Third International*, Petrograd, Soviet Union, 1920

Vladimir Tatlin and his assistants I.A. Meerzon and T.M. Shapiro constructing the first model for the *Monument to the Third International*, Petrograd, Soviet Union, 1920

Moscow showed laboratory-like material models (reliefs and counter-reliefs). An exhibition in 1917 presented examples of material combinations, which were the result of large-scale research and discoveries, dealing with the usage of materials in general and the resulting deductions of movement and tension, and the relation of one to the other.

Based on this research of material, volume, and construction, we were able, in 1918, to start combining materials such as iron and glass—the materials of modern classicism, which in their harshness can be compared to the marble of the classical world—into artistic forms. Thus we were able to combine pure, artistic forms with dedicated goals. One example is the design of a monument for the Third International, which was exhibited at the 8th Soviet Congress.

The results are models, encouraging inventions for our task of creating a new world and calling upon all artists to examine the forms that surround us in our daily lives.

Moscow, December 31, 1920

verlassen uns nicht mehr länger auf das Auge und bringen unsere Sinneseindrücke unter Kontrolle.

1915 wurde in Moskau eine Ausstellung mit laboratoriumsartigen Materialmodellen (Reliefs und Konterreliefs) veranstaltet. Auf einer 1917 gezeigten Ausstellung waren Beispiele von Materialkombinationen zu sehen, die das Ergebnis weitreichender Untersuchungen und Entdeckungen waren, und die Verwendung von Materialien an sich und die Folgerungen daraus betrafen, nämlich Bewegung, Spannung, und deren gegenseitiges Verhältnis zueinander.

Aufgrund dieser Untersuchungen von Material, Volumen und Konstruktion konnten wie 1918 an die Aufgabe gehen, Material wie Eisen oder Glas in künstlerischer Form zu kombinieren – also die Materialien des modernen Klassizismus, die in ihrer Strenge mit dem Marmor der Antike zu vergleichen sind. Auf diese Weise konnten wir reine, künstlerische Formen mit zweckbestimmten Zielsetzungen kombinieren. Ein Beispiel hierfür: Der Entwurf eines Denkmals zur III. Internationale, das zum 8. Sowjetkongress ausgestellt wurde.

Das Resultat sind Modelle, die uns bei unserer Arbeit am Aufbau einer neuen Welt zu neuen Entdeckungen anregen, und die alle Produzenten aufrufen, die Formen, die uns in unserem neuen Alltagsleben umgeben, zu untersuchen.

Moscow, 31. Dezember 1920

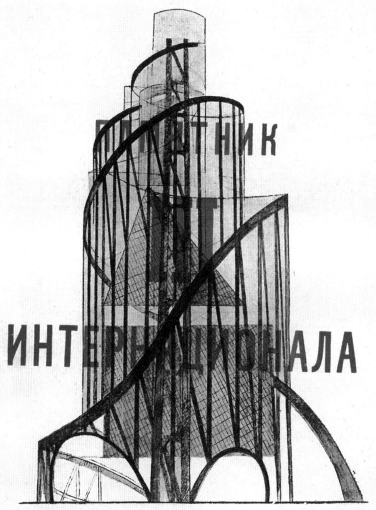

Н. ПУНИН

ПАМЯТНИК

ИНТЕРНАЦИОНАЛА

Проект худ. В. Е. ТАТЛИНА

ПЕТЕРБУРГ
Издание Отдела Изобразительных Искусств Н. К. П.
1920 г.

Cover of the *Monument to the Third International*, Nicolai Punin, Petrograd, 1920

Tatlin's Tower, Vision and Pretension, from 1917 onwards

Florian Medicus

Tatlins Turm, Vision und Anmaßung, 1917ff.

Florian Medicus

In coining the cultural concept of its time, Vladimir Yevgrafovich Tatlin's design for the *Monument to the Third International* can and should be seen as the most significant project of the Soviet avant-garde. It stands out from the somewhat confusing collective achievement of many ambitious projects for many different reasons but, ultimately, because it is symptomatic of the historical development of the young Soviet Union up to the year 1934.

In the weeks following the second successful coup of October 1917, the new Soviet government under Lenin had already started to rename important streets in Saint Petersburg after French revolutionary heroes of 1789 in order to proclaim a new society through means of identification. This shows what Lenin, Stalin and Lunacharsky called for in their so-called *Monumental Propaganda*—a visible break from the past

Wladimir Jewgrafowitsch Tatlins Entwurf für ein Monument der III. Internationalen kann und müsste eigentlich als das signifikanteste und wohl den Kulturbegriff der sowjetischen Avantgarde am stärksten prägende Projekt verstanden werden. Das Monument sticht aus einer vielfältigen, oft auch verwirrenden kollektiven Höchstleistung aus mehreren Gründen hervor, und steht letztlich symptomatisch für die geschichtliche Entwicklung der jungen Sowjetunion bis 1934.

Schon in den Wochen nach dem zweiten, geglückten Putsch im Oktober 1917 hatte die neue Sowjet-Verwaltung unter Lenin begonnen, wichtige Straßen in St. Petersburg nach französischen Revolutionshelden von 1789 zu benennen, um dem Versuch einer neuen Gesellschaftsordnung entsprechende Identifikationsmöglichkeiten bereitzustellen. Dieser Umstand beschreibt schon das fundamentale Verständnis dessen,

at all times, the use of new symbols for a new people and a firm conviction among the intelligentsia that their efforts would contribute decisively to the foundation of the new state and society.

By that time, Vladimir Tatlin had already become one of the most important figures of the Russian avant-garde, alongside Kazimir Malevich, who coined various concepts of art. His strange conflict with Malevich, and the increasing presence of Constructivism thanks to Rodchenko, in his work, came after the first vague concepts of Cubo-Futurism and Malevich's Suprematism. Unstable political and social circumstances and the devastating economic situation of the young Soviet Union did little harm to cultural production. It almost seems as though the sufferings of World War I and the later Civil War were simply ignored appurtenances of general propaganda. Strikingly, artists and intellectuals had united in committing themselves to the revolution of the working class, from which the new order of international socialism was supposed to emerge. The British historian Paul Wood refers indirectly to Karl Marx, according to whom utopia is converted into real science and calls this belief "materialistic idealism, which evolved out of a situation, in which utopia seemed to be deeply embedded in reality."[1]

Despite the collective, revolutionary approach of the time, artistic perceptions developed in various ways. This is clearly reflected in the diversity of art schools and unions, which also testify to the organisational, institutional, and theoretical efforts to advocate the development of this new life through the applied arts. At the beginning, the only spiritualized counter-concept to

was Lenin, Stalin und Lunatscharski 1918 in ihrer so genannten »Monumentalpropaganda« einforderten: den allzeit sichtbaren Bruch mit der zaristischen Vergangenheit, neue Bilder für neue Menschen und die feste Überzeugung aller Intelligenz, mit ihren Mitteln am Aufbau des neuen Staates und der neuen Gesellschaft entscheidend mitzuwirken.

Wladimir Tatlin war zu dieser Zeit neben Kasimir Malewitsch zur prägenden und für die verschiedenen Kunstauffassungen der russischen Avantgarde so wesentlichen Figur aufgestiegen; sein sonderbares Zerwürfnis mit (dem weniger politischen) Malewitsch und die fortschreitende Profilierung des Konstruktivismus durch Rodtschenko folgten dem noch etwas verschwommenen Ansatz des Kubo-Futurismus und Malewitschs Suprematismus nach. Instabile politische und soziale Umstände taten dabei dem kulturellen Schaffen jedoch ebenso wenig Abbruch, wie die verheerende wirtschaftliche Situation der jungen Sowjetunion. Fast scheint es, als waren die Entbehrungen des Weltkrieges und späteren Bürgerkrieges weitgehend ignoriertes Beiwerk der allgemeinen Propaganda. Künstler und Intellektuelle hatten sich auffällig geschlossen der Revolution der Arbeiterklasse verschrieben, aus der die neue Ordnung des internationalen Sozialismus entstehen sollte. Der britische Historiker Paul Wood verweist hierbei indirekt auf Karl Marx, wonach Utopie in reale Wissenschaft überführt wurde und nennt diesen Umstand den »materialistischen Idealismus, der aus einer Situation hervorging, in der die Utopie tief in die Wirklichkeit eingegraben zu sein schien«.[1]

Reconstruction of Tatlin's *Complex Corner Relief*, 1915, Martyn Chalk

eclecticism and Art Nouveau was founded primarily on French Cubism, Italian Futurism, and its Russian version, Cubo-Futurism (1912/13–1916). Nevertheless, proponents soon split up into two schools, which again used Suprematism (K. Malevich, E. Lissitzky, L. Popowa et al., (UNOVIS) Vitebsk) and Constructivism (V. Tatlin, A. Rodchenko, N. Gabo et al., (INChUK) Moscow and Petrograd) as two defining approaches.

Suprematism already defined itself as a rejection of the Cubistic experiment and had a great influence on the Central European avant-garde in the Netherlands and Germany, mainly through El Lissitzky. Both schools (Vitebsk and Moscow) dealt mainly with the formal-aesthetic problems at the intersection of art and architecture that excluded a functional debate (which Lenin had originally demanded with regard to the general housing situation). A few years later, Lissitzky noted "a new asymmetrical balance built, the tension of bodies brought to a new dynamic expression, and new rhythmic positioned."[2]

In Vitebsk, artists were more interested in the artistic possibilities of strictly geometrical expression. Architecture was understood as an integral part of art, but reduced to a problem of pure forms and detached from constructive and functional factors. This was different to Tatlin's approach in Moscow (and from mid-1919 in Petrograd again), whose studio "Volumes, Material, and Construction" mainly focused on material texture, the connection of high contrast materials, and new constructive forms. Lissitzky states: "The leader of this movement (Tatlin) assumed that the intuitive artistic mastery of material leads to inventions, in which objects can be built, regard-

Wie unterschiedlich sich die Kunstauffassungen trotz des kollektiven, revolutionären Ansatzes entwickelten, sieht man am deutlichsten an den vielen Kunstschulen und Vereinen, die ein unmittelbares Zeugnis des organisatorischen, institutionellen wie auch theoretischen Engagements ablegen, in angewandter Kunst(-praxis) für Aufbau und Gestaltung des neuen Lebens einzutreten. Das zuerst nur vergeistigte Gegenmodell zu Eklektizismus und Jugendstil gründete mehrheitlich auf den französischen Kubismus, italienischen Futurismus (Marinetti trug 1914 den »futuristischen Weg« in St. Petersburg vor) und seine russische Synthese, den Kubo-Futurismus (1912/13–1916). Dieser allerdings zerschlug sich bald in mehrere Strömungen und Schulen, die wiederum den Suprematismus (K. Malewitsch, E. Lissitzky, L. Popowa u.a., [UNOVIS] Witebsk) und den Konstruktivismus (W. Tatlin, A. Rodtschenko, N. Gabo u.a., [INChUK] Moskau und Petrograd) als prägende Hauptrichtungen einsetzten. Der Suprematismus empfand sich bereits als Ergebnis der Ablehnung des kubistischen Experiments und hatte vor allem durch die verbindende Wirkung El Lissitzkys großen Einfluss auf die mitteleuropäische Avantgarde in Holland und Deutschland. Beide Schulen (Witebsk und Moskau) beschäftigten sich vornehmlich mit formal-ästhetischen Problemen an der Schnittstelle von bildender Kunst und Architektur, was eine funktionelle Debatte (wie sie Lenin etwa im Bezug auf die allgemeine Wohnsituation gefordert hatte) ausschloss. Lissitzky sah einige Jahre später »ein neues asymmetrisches Gleichgewicht aufgebaut, die Spannungen der Körper zu einem neuen dynamischen Ausdruck gebracht und eine neue

less of the rational scientific methods of technology. He believes he proves this in his design for the *Monument to the Third International*."[3]

Vladimir Tatlin originally aimed at creating a new valid basis for painting and seeking, with his counter-reliefs, Cubist transformations in three dimensions. While at about the same time, Marcel Duchamp worked on his *Bicycle Wheel* and *Bottle Rack*, in which he left the ready-made objects in their isolated, absolute condition, Tatlin sorted his finds according to material syntheses. Each object could, if detached from its original state, be seen as material. This included far more than only the collage technique used by the Cubists.[4]

Tatlin's design for the *Monument to the Third International* is seen by many as a logical continuation of his (counter)-reliefs on a larger scale. Tatlin himself saw this connection, which he explained through the term "material-form."[5] Nonetheless, the tower marks a caesura in Vladimir Tatlin's artistic work and was also to divide the era of the avant-garde into two periods, that is, "before" and "after" the monument. The revolution simply called for new symbols and new arguments with respect to the present and future, as well as authentic and, even more importantly, valid aesthetic contributions to the success of the great plan. The pretentious attitude of one's own theoretical and practical grandiosity combined with the latent ignorance of the quite obvious circumstances of production represented an important aspect in this project. In the post-revolutionary fervor, everything seemed possible, everything new, and the wide field of possibilities open for unrestricted optimism as well as for a genuine

Rhythmik aufgestellt«.[2] In Witebsk interessierte man sich vermehrt für die künstlerischen Möglichkeiten im reduzierten, streng geometrischen Ausdruck. Architektur wurde zwar als integraler Bestandteil der Kunst begriffen, allerdings reduziert auf ein reines Formproblem und losgelöst von konstruktiven oder funktionalen Faktoren. Einen anderen Ansatz findet man bei Tatlin in Moskau (und ab Mitte 1919 wieder in Petrograd), dessen Studio »Volumen, Material und Konstruktion« sich im Wesentlichen dem ästhetischen Ausdruck in der Textur des Materials, der Verbindung kontrastreicher Werkstoffe und neuen konstruktiven Formen widmete. Bei Lissitzky liest man: »Der Führer dieser Bewegung (Tatlin) nahm an, dass die intuitiv künstlerische Beherrschung des Materials zu Erfindungen führte, auf deren Grundlage sich Gegenstände aufbauen lassen, unabhängig von den rationell wissenschaftlichen Methoden der Technik. Er glaubte dies in seinem Entwurf für das Denkmal der III. Internationalen zu beweisen.«[3] Wladimir Tatlin war ursprünglich bemüht gewesen, eine neue, gültige Basis für die Malerei zu schaffen und mit seinen Kontra-Reliefs ab 1913 kubistische Transformationen in die dritte Dimension zu ermöglichen. Während Marcel Duchamp etwa zeitgleich sein *Bicycle Wheel* und den *Flaschentrockner* erarbeitete und die Ready-Made-Objects in ihrem isolierten, absoluten Zustand beließ, ordnete Tatlin seine Fundstücke zu Materialsynthesen. Jedes Objekt konnte, wenn es aus seinem ursprünglichen Zusammenhang herausgelöst wird, als Material aufgefasst werden. Dies beinhaltete weit mehr als nur die Collagetechnik, die die Kubisten anwendeten.[4]

The Confusion of Tongues, Gustave Doré, 1865

belief in the possibility of completely restructuring human culture. An article entitled the "Problem of Artistic Education" published in 1920 states: "The time is drawing near when the proletariat will need gigantic buildings, which are able to accommodate tens of thousands of people. A minimum development of force, a minimum of material, a maximum of constructiveness—this is the building law of the proletariat."[6]

In the spring of 1919, Vladimir Tatlin was commissioned by the People's Commissariat for Education under Anatoly Lunacharsky to design a monument to the Third International that would be fitting of the times. It is assumed that he already had his first inkling at the end of 1918, when he was still actively participating in the organisation, but not any idea of the design, of the "Monumental Propaganda." Two drawings exist from that time, which differ drastically from his first model in 1920. The ease and transparency of his original idea—with its clear focus on the spirals (the most prominent symbol of the revolution), supported by the skewed backbone of the building and the free-hanging geometrical bodies—were lost as design features. Tatlin's *process plastic*[8] necessarily shows an emergent machine, a compacted propaganda apparatus. The spirals lost their supporting function in the model, which was completely taken over by vertical and skewed elements that, contrary to the original idea, led to a clear definition between inside and outside (a fact that made Tatlin present a reworked version in 1925 in Paris, about which unfortunately little is known.) The open spatial construction, which should have contained four gigantic rotating volumes, each representing buildings of their

Tatlins Entwurf für das Monument der III. Internationalen wird von verschiedenen Seiten als schlüssige Fortsetzung der (Kontra-)Reliefs in größerem Maßstab gesehen; Tatlin selbst sah den Zusammenhang im Terminus der »Material-Form« erklärt.[5] Der Turm markiert jedenfalls eine Zäsur in Wladimir Tatlins künstlerischem Schaffen, wie er überhaupt die Epoche der Avantgarde in ein *Vor* und *Nach* dem Monument teilen sollte (siehe das später wiederkehrende, dynamisch-asymmetrische Turmmotiv bei A. Rodtschenko, N. Gabo u.a.). Die Revolution forderte schlichtweg neue Sinnbilder, Argumente der Gegenwart und Zukunft, glaubwürdige und mehr noch: ästhetisch verpflichtende Beiträge zum Gelingen des großen Plans. Das Festhalten an der eigenen, theoretischen wie praktischen Großartigkeit gemeinsam mit der latenten Ignoranz der eigentlich unübersehbaren Produktionsmissstände stellte gerade in diesem Projekt einen signifikanten Faktor dar. Im Jetzt des postrevolutionären Verständnisses war alles möglich, alles neu und das weite Feld der Wahrscheinlichkeiten noch offen für uneingeschränkten Optimismus und den wohl tatsächlich empfundenen Glauben an die völlige Neustrukturierung der menschlichen Kultur. Und so war in einem Artikel zur »Problematik der künstlerischen Ausbildung« war 1920 zu lesen: »Es naht die Zeit, da das Proletariat gewaltige Gebäude brauchen wird, die mehrere zehntausend Menschen aufnehmen. Minimale Kraftentfaltung, minimale Materialmenge, maximale Konstruktivität – das ist das Baugesetz der Gebäude des Proletariats.«[6]

Im Frühjahr 1919 wurde Wladimir Tatlin also seitens des Volkskommissariats

own, and the spiral threads' dramatic dynamic with the tilt of the basic supporting structure, suggests that Tatlin could not and also obviously did not care about static or functional principles. It is thus even more striking that a commission of engineers and architects agreed in 1919 that the monument could be built with the technology available at that time.[9]

It is highly speculative and ultimately futile to measure the tower's repetitive and actually possible iconography on the one hand and to ponder probabilities on the other. It is ultimately also irrelevant to know if the Tower of Babel, the Eiffel Tower, the Malwiya Minaret in Samarra, Rodin's Tower of Work, Hermann Obricht's monument design or Johannes Kepler's World Machine from 1596 were realized in keeping with their respective time and space. It seems more important to point out what Moisei Ginzburg described as the main factors of the new style a few years later: monumentality, asymmetry, and dynamic,[10] in close connection with the modern means of production and the implementation of technological accomplishments. All these demands were fulfilled in Tatlin's design on a gigantic scale—there was even talk of so-called "Thermos" walls (containing voids of air in between them) that should have enabled different rooms to maintain the same temperature.[11]

The last cited text by Nicolai Punin from March 9th, 1919 is also remarkable in terms of its function. Not only does it state that Tatlin had realized the complete synthesis between the different forms of art, but that he was also to create a propagandistic machine of projection towards the inside (agitation) as well as the outside

für Bildungswesen unter Anatoli Lunatscharski beauftragt, der III. Internationalen (Komintern) ein den zeitlichen Umständen entsprechendes Denkmal zu entwerfen. Die ersten Ideen dazu dürften ihm schon Ende des Jahres 1918 gekommen sein, als Tatlin noch sehr aktiv im organisatorischen, nicht jedoch im entwerfenden Bereich der »Monumentalpropaganda« mitwirkte. Aus dieser Zeit stammen jedenfalls die beiden Zeichnungen, die sich vom ersten Modell aus dem Jahr 1920 empfindlich unterschieden. Die ursprüngliche Leichtigkeit und Transparenz, mit dem klaren Fokus auf die durch das schräg gestellte Rückgrat gestützten Spiralen (das Symbol der Revolution schlechthin)[7] und den frei hängenden geometrischen Körpern war als Gestaltungsmerkmal verloren gegangen. Tatlins *process plastic*[8] zeigt notwendigerweise eine in sich werdende Maschine, einen verdichteten Propagandaapparat; die Spiralen verloren im Modell ihre tragende Funktion, die völlig von senkrechten und schrägen Elementen übernommen wurde, was dazu führte, dass entgegen der ursprünglichen Idee ein klares Innen und Außen definiert wurde (ein Umstand, der Tatlin 1925 eine überarbeitete Version in Paris präsentieren ließ, von der leider nur wenig bekannt ist). Die offene Raumkonstruktion, in der sich also vier gewaltige Volumina, letztlich selbständige Gebäude drehen sollten, die kühne Dynamik der Spiralgewinde mitsamt der Schrägstellung der grundlegenden Tragkonstruktion konnte sich nicht um statische oder gar funktionale Prinzipien kümmern und wollte das ganz offensichtlich auch nicht. Umso bemerkenswerter, dass eine eigens eingesetzte Kommission aus

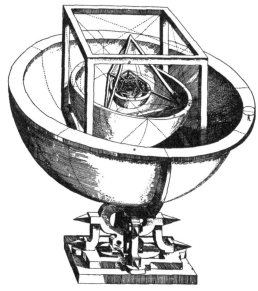

Solar Model, Johannes Kepler, c.1597

Turris Babel, Livius Creyl and Athanasius Kircher, 1670

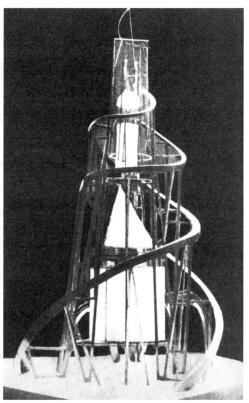

Later Model of the *Monument to the Third International*,
Vladimir Tatlin, Paris, 1925

Tatlin's Tower, Vision and Pretension, from 1917 onwards   59

(radio station, illuminated letters in the sky), in which "people should stand or sit as little as possible."[12] The monument thus combined everything demanded by dogma and even surpassed it in some areas. Its formal and textual dynamics, its spirit as an advanced (world) machine, its function that closely followed the official party line, and its extraordinary, almost egomaniacal scale, clearly represented the newly founded superpower.

Finally, I would like to allude to a perhaps confusing dimension of Tatlin's work, which has also been touched upon independently by Adolf Max Vogt, John Milner, and, later, also Anatoly Strigalyov—namely Tatlin's cosmism. In the jubilation over the successful revolution and the newly emerging worker state, Leo Trotzky stated: "In cosmism, the perception is thus that we should see the whole world as a coherent whole and ourselves as an active part of it, so that in the future we can not only rule the world, but the whole cosmos. All this is of course magnificent, wonderful and superb. Once our home was confined to Kursk and Kalug, a short time ago we conquered Russia and now we are marching towards world revolution. And now should we be stopped by the confines of our planet?"[13] Vogt, Milner, and later also Strigalyov note in Tatlin's monument a concordance with the 23.5° tilt of the earth's axis not only in the way that the agitation volumes inside should have rotated, but also in the exact tilt of its "spine." A motive, which was implemented by Vogt, Lissitzky, Leonidov and others up until Le Corbusier's design for the Soviet Palace of 1931. It may also be significant that Petrograd (today Saint Petersburg again) was the Russian center of astronomical studies at that time. The

Ingenieuren und Architekten noch 1919 dahingehend urteilte, dass »das gegenwärtige Niveau der Technik die Ausführung des Bauwerks in vollem Maße möglich macht«.[9]

Es scheint hochspekulativ und letztlich unsinnig, die stets wiederkehrende und tatsächlich mögliche Ikonografie des Turms abzuleiten und gleichsam in Wahrscheinlichkeiten abzuwägen. Ob der Turmbau zu Babel, Eiffelturm, das Malwiya-Minarett in Samarra, Rodins *Turm der Arbeit*, Hermann Obrichts Denkmal-Entwurf oder sogar Johannes Keplers 1596 erdachte *Weltmaschine* hier ihre ort- und zeitgemäße Umsetzung erfuhren, ist letztlich auch unwesentlich. Dringlicher scheint es auf die Grundlagen dessen hinzuweisen, was Moisej Ginzburg einige Jahre später als die wesentlichen Faktoren des neuen Stils beschrieb: Monumentalität, Asymmetrie und Dynamik[10], und dies in enger Verbindung mit modernen Produktionsmitteln und Nutzung der technischen Errungenschaften. All diese Forderungen sieht man in Tatlins Entwurf in gewaltigem Maßstab erfüllt; sogar so genannte »Thermos« (Wände mit luftleerem Raum dazwischen) wurden besprochen, die es ermöglichen sollten, die Temperatur in den verschiedenen Räumen gleichmäßig zu halten.[11]

Der zuletzt zitierte Text von Nicolai Punin vom 9. März 1919 ist jedoch auch in funktionaler Hinsicht bemerkenswert. Nicht nur, dass Tatlin die vollendete Synthese zwischen den verschiedenen Formen der Kunst gelungen sei, sondern es sollte hier auch eine propagandistische Projektionsmaschine nach Innen (Agitation) wie nach Außen (Radiosender, Leuchtbuchstaben in den Himmel) entstehen, »in der so wenig wie möglich herumgestanden oder

Hermitage commanded various measuring instruments and documents regarding this topic, making Milner's analogy of Tatlin's monument an oversized telescope, which he draws in his reflection, comprehensible. Another indication can be found in Lissitzky's portrait of Tatlin (*At Work*, 1922): Here, Tatlin is likewise identified with a compass and with the mathematical symbols for the helix and eternity.

Since its declaration of intent, the monument has generated huge interest and enthusiasm but also criticism among different artist groups and political circles. In his report from 1973, for example, Kyrill Afanasjev attributes "the crudity of the tower's constructive forms" to Tatlin's "technical illiteracy or the deliberate disdain of engineering knowledge."[14] Afanasjev cites the engineer Vladimir Shukhov, whose radio tower was actually realized in 1922, despite severe difficulties in procuring materials, as an example that counters Tatlin's "emotional constructivism." Without wanting to deny Shukhov my complete admiration, in concluding, I would nevertheless like to take issue with Kyrill Afanasjev. Compared to Tatlin's monument, Shukhov's exceptional talent did, of course, manifest itself better under the difficult circumstances of production; yet, we also need to ask whether we can compare the monuments at all. It would be similarly strange to compare between the fuel consumption of a VW Polo and an Aston Martin DB9: both are vehicles on four wheels—but with very different goals and expectations. During his lifetime, Vladimir Tatlin also seems to have pursued different goals than others, when he formulated his motto, "painting + engineering – architecture = material construction

gesessen werden soll«.[12] Das Monument verband also in diesem Zusammenhang alles dogmatisch Geforderte, übertraf es sogar stellenweise: formale und inhaltliche Dynamik, den Geist der fortschrittlichen (Welt-)Maschine und die parteikonforme Funktion in einem selbstherrlichen, nahezu irrwitzigen Maßstab der eben erst begründeten Supermacht.

Abschließend sei noch auf einen, möglicherweise zusätzlich verwirrenden Umstand hingewiesen, der, wie ich denke, unabhängig voneinander bei Adolf Max Vogt und etwas später bei John Milner auftaucht: Tatlins Kosmismus. In dem Jubel über die geglückte Revolution und den zusehends sich festigenden Arbeiterstaat formulierte Leo Trotzki: »Im ›Kosmismus‹ ist die Vorstellung etwa die, dass man die ganze Welt als eine gewisse Einheit empfinden sollte und sich selbst als einen aktiven Teil davon, mit der Aussicht künftig nicht nur die Erde allein, sondern auch den ganzen Kosmos beherrschen zu können. All das ist natürlich sehr prächtig und wunderbar wie großartig. Einst begrenzte sich unsere Heimat auf Kursk und Kaluga, vor kurzem haben wir Russland erobert und schreiten nun zur Weltrevolution. Und da sollen wir uns von den Grenzen unseres Planeten aufhalten lassen?«[13] Beide, Vogt und Milner – später auch Anatoli Strigaljow – sehen nicht nur in der Art, wie sich die Agitationsvolumen im Inneren hätten drehen sollen, sondern in der Exaktheit der Schrägneigung des »Rückgrats« von Tatlins Monument eine Übereinstimmung mit der 23,5°-Schrägneigung der Erdachse. Ein Motiv anbei, das nach Vogt bei Lissitzky, Leonidov bis hin zu Le Corbusiers Entwurf für den Sowjet-Palast von 1931 Eingang fand. Vielleicht

Model of the *Monument to the Third International*, Vladimir Tatlin (in front), Petrograd, 1920

(a + c−o = k)."[15] Eiffel had built in Paris and thus materialised and proved the industrial spirit of his time. Nevertheless, gravity, new building materials, and methods (Trotzky called the Eiffel Tower not a construction but a simple construction exercise)[16] had not been challenged or even conquered. Ever since, material idealism has granted various exceptional projects a certain indestructibility, which is and probably always will be distinct to them as symbols of the twentieth century revolution, even despite the historical defeat of the avant-garde's social and cultural vision.

1   Paul Wood in *Die große Utopie*, exhibition catalogue, Frankfurt: Schirn Art Hall, 1992, pp.283ff.
2   El Lissitzky, *Architektur für eine Weltrevolution*, Vienna: Verlag Anton Schroll, 1930, p.11.
3   Lissitzky 1930, p.11.
4   Troels Andersen, *Wladimir Tatlin 1885–1953*, Munich: Art Society, 1970, pp.6–7.
5   Cf. Anatoly Strigalyov, *Tatlin*: Weingarten Verlag, 1987, pp.30ff.
6   Strigalyov, 1987, p.31.
7   Kyrill Afanasjew, *Ideen, Projekte, Bauten*, Dresden: Verlag der Kunst, 1973, p.11.
8   John Milner, *Tatlin and the Russian Avant-Garde*, New Haven and London: Yale University Press, 1983, pp.151ff.
9   Cf. Strigalyov 1987, p.34.
10   Moisei Ginzburg, *Stil und Epoche*, 1924.
11   Nicolai Punin, "Veshch Nr. 1–2, Berlin 1922" in Andersen 1970, p.49.
12   Nicolai Punin, "Iskusstwo kommuni, Petrograd 1919" in Andersen 1970, p.48.
13   Cited in Adolf Max Vogt, *Revolutionsarchitektur, 1917–1789*, Cologne: Dumont, 1974, p.215.
14   Afanasjev, 1973, p.12.
15   Cf. Strigalyov, 1987, p.39.
16   Leo Trotzky, *Literatur und Revolution*, 1924 in Andersen 1970, p.53.

spielte es auch eine Rolle, dass Petrograd (heute wieder St. Petersburg) zur damaligen Zeit das russische Zentrum für astronomische Studien war; die Eremitage verfügte über allerhand Messgeräte und Unterlagen zu diesem Thema und so ist auch die Analogie mit einem überdimensionalen Teleskop verständlich, wie sie Milner in seiner Betrachtung zieht. Ein weiteres Indiz findet sich bei Lissitzkys Portrait von Tatlin (Tatlin bei der Arbeit, 1922, Abb. S.40): Tatlin wird mit einem Kompass ebenso assoziiert, wie mit den mathematischen Symbolen für Spirale und Unendlichkeit.

Das Monument sorgte seit der ersten Absichtserklärung für reges Interesse, für Begeisterung und ebenso vehemente Ablehnung innerhalb der Künstlergruppen und darüber hinaus in politischen Kreisen. In seinem 1973 erschienenen Bericht unterstellt beispielsweise Kyrill Afanasjew Tatlin »technischen Analphabetismus oder vorsätzliche Geringschätzung der Ingenieurkenntnisse, die zur Ungeschliffenheit der konstruktiven Formen des Turmes führten«.[14] Afanasjew führt gegen den »emotionalen Konstruktivismus« Tatlins den Ingenieur Wladimir Schuchov an, dass dessen Funkturm 1922 tatsächlich, wenn auch mit größten Schwierigkeiten in der Materialbeschaffung, errichtet werden konnte. Ohne Schuchov die umfassende Bewunderung vorenthalten zu wollen, würde ich Kyrill Afanasjew abschließend gerne widersprechen. Schuchovs außergewöhnliche Begabung konnte sich im Rahmen der schwierigen Produktionsumstände natürlich eher materialisieren als Tatlins Monument, wobei hier die Fragwürdigkeit des Vergleichs an sich gestellt sei. Ebenso

Design for a City with "Elevated Façades", Alexander Rodchenko, 1920

sonderbar würde ein zeitgemäßer Vergleich im Treibstoffverbrauch zwischen einem VW Polo und dem Aston Martin DB9 anmuten; beides Fahrzeuge auf vier Rädern gewiss: nur eben ganz anderen Zielen und Erwartungen gewidmet. Und ebenso dürfte Wladimir Tatlin zeitlebens andere Ziele verfolgt haben, wenn er seine Losung »Malerei + Ingenieurwissenschaften – Architektur = Materialkonstruktion $(a + c - o = k)$«[15] formulierte. Eiffel hatte in Paris gebaut, den industrialisierten Zeitgeist materialisiert und somit bewiesen: Die Schwerkraft, neue Baumaterialien und -methoden jedoch waren damit (Trotzki bezeichnete den Eiffelturm abschätzig nicht als Bau, sondern als reine Bauübung)[16] noch lange nicht ausreichend herausgefordert oder gar überwunden. Der schon erwähnte materialistische Idealismus jedenfalls verleiht den vielen außergewöhnlichen Projekten und dem Besprochenen im Besonderen seither selbst auf der Basis der historischen Niederlage der gesellschaftlichen und kulturellen Vision der Avantgarde eine Unverwüstlichkeit, die ihnen als Sinnbilder der Revolution des 20. Jahrhunderts eigen ist und vermutlich auch bleiben wird.

1   Paul Wood in *Die große Utopie*; Katalog zur Ausstellung, Schirn Kunsthalle Frankfurt, 1992; S.283ff.
2   El Lissitzky in *Architektur für eine Weltrevolution*, Verlag Anton Schroll, Wien; 1930; S.11.
3   Lissitzky, 1930; S.11.
4   Troels Andersen in *Wladimir Tatlin 1885–1953*, Kunstverein München, 1970; S.6f.
5   nach Anatoli Strigaljow in *Tatlin*, Weingarten Verlag, 1987; S.30ff.
6   Strigaljow, 1987; S.31.
7   Kyrill Afanasjew in *Ideen – Projekte – Bauten*, Verlag der Kunst Dresden, 1973; S.11.
8   John Milner in *Tatlin and the Russian Avant-Garde*, Yale University Press, 1983; S.151ff.
9   nach Anatoli Strigaljow in *Tatlin*, Weingarten Verlag, 1987; S.34.
10 Moisej Ginzburg in *Stil und Epoche*, 1924.
11 Nicolai Punin in »Veshch Nr. 1–2«, Berlin 1922; in *Wladimir Tatlin 1885–1953*, S.49.
12 Nicolai Punin in »Iskusstwo kommuni, Petrograd 1919«; in *Wladimir Tatlin 1885–1953*, S.48.
13 Leo Trotzki nach Adolf Max Vogt in *Revolutionsarchitektur 1917–1789*, DuMont, Köln, 1974; S.215.
14 Kyrill Afanasjew in *Ideen – Projekte – Bauten*, Verlag der Kunst Dresden, 1973; S.12.
15 nach Anatoli Strigaljow in *Tatlin*, Weingarten Verlag, 1987; S.39.
16 Leo Trotzki in »Literatur und Revolution«, 1924 in *Wladimir Tatlin 1885–1953*, S.53.

Verwendete und weiterführende Literatur:

Afanasjew, Kyrill N.; Ideen-Projekte-Bauten; Fundus (VEB), Dresden, 1973.
Altrichter, Helmut; *Kleine Geschichte der Sowjetunion 1917–1991*; beck'sche reihe, München, 1993.
Andersen, Troels; *Tatlin* (Katalog Stockholm, Eindhoven, Delft, München); Moderna Museet Stockholm, 1968.
Chan-Magomedow, Selim O.; *Russisch-sowjetische Architektur 1900–1923*; DVA, Stuttgart, 1991.
Chan-Magomedow, Selim O.; *Pioniere der sowjetischen Architektur*; Verlag der Kunst, Dresden, 1983.
Cooke, Catherine; *Russian Avant-Garde*; Academy Editions, London, 1995.
Cooke, Catherine; *Architectural Drawings of the Russian Avant-Garde*; MOMA, New York, 1990.
Gray, Camilla; *The Russian Experiment in Art*, Thames& Hudson, London, 1962 (Neuauflage 2000).
Harten, Jürgen (Hg.); *Tatlin – Leben, Werk, Wirkung*; DuMont, Köln, 1993.
Harten, Jürgen und Strigalev, Anatolij; *Vladimir Tatlin – Retrospektive*; DuMont, Köln, 1993.
Lissitzky, El; »Russland – Architektur für eine Weltrevolution«; (Wien, 1930) *Bauwelt Fundamente* 1965.
Lissitzky, El; *Proun und Wolkenbügel*; Fundus (VEB), Dreden, 1977.
Milner, John; *Vladimir Tatlin and the Russian Avant-Garde*; Yale University Press, New Haven, 1983.
Noever, Peter bzw. Néray, Katalin; *Art and Revolution*, MAK, Wien, 1988.
Shadowa, Larissa (Hg.); *Tatlin*; Kunstverlag Weingarten, 1987.
Vogt, Adolf Max; *Revolutionsarchitektur 1789–1917*; DuMont, Köln, 1974.
Wolter, Bettina-Martine und Schwenk, Bernhard; *Die große Utopie*; Schirn Kunsthalle, Frankfurt, 1992.

ФАСАД

МАСШТАБ 1 500

Drawing of Tatlin's Tower

The Curved Line as Form, Metaphor, and Policy

Gabriele Werner

Die gekrümmte Linie als Form, Metapher und Politik

Gabriele Werner

As to be expected with such a spectacular vision, Vladimir Tatlin's design for his *Monument to the Third International* (1919–1920) is the subject of many different art theories with distinct motivations and means of interpretation. Sometimes, with and against the (still Russian) formalistic school, and in the sense of a formal art historical analysis, the "graphic" means of the straight and curved lines of the exterior framework are at the center of a description. From an art historical perspective with a focus on social history, the structure is highlighted as a futuristic monument of Soviet industrial modernity. Finally, it is also often seen as an example of the Soviet Union's materialized, revolutionary politics, not yet identified with Stalinist totalitarianism, but with a Leninist social, and thus also artistic, utopia. From today's point of view, it certainly makes sense to keep two things in mind. In 1919, only two

Wladimir Tatlins Entwurf für ein Denkmal der Dritten Internationale (1919–1920) ist, wie sollte es anders sein bei solch einer spektakulären Vision, Gegenstand ganz unterschiedlich motivierter Kunsttheorien und damit Deutungsversuche. Mit und gegen die (noch russische) formalistische Schule und im Sinne einer kunsthistorischen Formanalyse stehen einmal die »grafischen« Mittel der geraden und gekrümmten Linien des Außengerüsts im Mittelpunkt der Beschreibung. Ein weiteres Mal wird der Baukörper in einer sozialgeschichtlich ausgerichteten Kunstgeschichte als futuristisches Monument der industriellen, sowjetischen Moderne hervorgehoben und zu guter Letzt steht das Denkmal immer auch für eine materiell gewordene, revolutionäre Politik der Sowjetunion, die noch nicht mit dem stalinistischen Totalitarismus identifiziert wird, sondern mit einer leninistischen

years after the October Revolution, art and politics were in an experimental phase. Futurism, Formalism, Constructivism and Productivism were fiercely competing over how best to serve the revolution and debating which new forms should be used to give this new society a face. A model of Tatlin's monument was indeed exhibited in 1920 in Petrograd and later also in Moscow, but it never made it past the design or idea stage. However, the model itself and, even more so, the drawings of it, show that its many ambiguities are exactly what make a reconstruction so appealing.

How many different interpretations already existed even among Tatlin's contemporaries is best shown by the comments of, on the one hand, the art historian Nicolay Punin, at that time still a Tatlin supporter and on the other, Viktor Shklovsky, the theoretician of Russian Futurism and head of the formalistic school. Punin published a pamphlet in the paper *Art and Commune* under the heading "Communism and Futurism" in March 1919, in which he refers, among other things, to Tatlin's Monument to the Third International, analogizing its form with the Comintern's goals. Punin stated that the Third International further developed the inclination of the Second and especially the First International to move "straight out of these 'spatial axes' around which people of past times had built their countries." As he elaborated, "Spatio-national territories crumble; territories of time develop into a uniform, leveled space, which is covered by the international Proletariat. Is this not the new, not our futuristic form?"[1] Reference here is made particularly to the space-embracing spiral form and the tilt of the exterior frame parallel to the

Sozialutopie und damit auch mit einer Kunstutopie. Gewiss ist es sinnvoll, aus der heutigen Distanz zweierlei zu berücksichtigen: 1919, also gerade mal zwei Jahre nach der Oktoberrevolution, befanden sich Kunst und Politik in der Experimentierphase. Futurismus, Formalismus, Konstruktivismus, Produktivismus befanden sich im heftigen Wettstreit um den Dienst an der Revolution und um die neuen Formen, mit der die neue Gesellschaft ihr Gesicht erhalten sollte. Zudem wurde zwar 1920 ein Modell des Denkmals in Petrograd und danach in Moskau ausgestellt, aber selbst dieses Modell und erst recht die Zeichnungen zeigen deutlich, dass das Denkmal über das Stadium eines Entwurfs, also einer Idee, nicht hinausgegangen ist – und die vielen Uneindeutigkeiten ja genau den Anreiz für die Rekonstruktionsversuche ausmachen.

Wie weit sich der Bogen der Interpretation schon unter den Zeitgenossen Tatlins spannte, verdeutlichen die Äußerungen des Kunsthistorikers und zu dem Zeitpunkt noch Tatlin-Befürworters Nicolai Punin einerseits und des Theoretikers des russischen Futurismus und Kopf der formalistischen Schule Wiktor Schklowski andererseits. Unter der Überschrift »Kommunismus und Futurismus« veröffentlichte Punin im März 1919 in der Zeitschrift *Kunst und Kommune* eine Streitschrift, in der er sich unter anderem auf Tatlins Denkmal für die Dritte Internationale bezieht und seine Form mit den Zielen der Komintern analogisiert, führe doch die dritte Internationale, indem sie die Richtung der zweiten, und besonders der ersten Internationale weiterentwickle, »gerade aus jenen ›Raumachsen‹ hinaus, um die herum die Menschen der Vergangenheit ihre Staaten bauten.

earth's axis. Viktor Shklovsky, Punin's counterpart in this debate on principles within the Russian Futuristic movement about the "formal content and the ontological status of artistic creation", avoids a metaphorical interpretation of the monument in his account. "For the first time iron rears up and wants to assume its artistic mission", writes Shklovsky, in keeping with Tatlin's manifesto of material culture, which attributes interior material forces to the form of the exterior curvature. And so also its subject, the Council of the People's Commissars, is a new material "which, united with Rosta, is used for constructing the artistic form."[2]

The iron and steel works, Rosta, as a place of industrial development, is merged with the form of an upward striving spiral and gives the politics of the Communist International its form. So the debate proceeded along the lines of whether revolutionary art would commit itself to social reality, where its form would be more or less arbitrary, or whether art through its forms would create content, where "reality" would be seen as yet undesigned material, which only art would be able to accord specific visibility.

That the aesthetic positions in this art debate are deeply political is emphasized by both contemporary and subsequent comments on the monument's functionality.

In his main work on literary criticism *Literature and Revolution* from 1923, Leo Trotzky regards the steel frame as much too labored and the monument for the Comintern as a pure temple of staging. For him, it is self-evident that committee conferences should not to be held in a cylinder, even less in one that rotates and is made of glass.[3] Evidently however, this objection did

Räumlich-nationale Territorien zerfallen, es entstehen Territorien der Zeit bei einheitlichem, nivelliertem Raum, der vom internationalen Proletariat bedeckt wird. Ist das etwa nicht die neue, nicht unsere futuristische Form?«[1] Bezug genommen wird hier vor allem auf die den Raum umfassende Spiralform und die Neigung des äußeren Baukörpers parallel zur Erdachse. Punins Gegenüber in der Grundsatzdiskussion innerhalb der russischen futuristischen Bewegung um »den formalen Gehalt und den ontologischen Status des künstlerischen Schaffens«, Wiktor Schklowski, vermeidet in seiner Darstellung, das Denkmal metaphorisch zu deuten: »Zum ersten Mal bäumt das Eisen sich auf und will seine künstlerische Formel annehmen« schreibt Schklowski, ganz im Sinne von Tatlins Programm einer Materialkultur, nach der die Bogenlinien die inneren Materialkräfte veräußerlichen, und so sei auch sein Gegenstand selbst, der Rat der Volkskommissare, ein neues Material, »das, vereint mit der Rosta, zur Konstruktion der künstlerischen Form benutzt wird.«[2] Die Eisen- und Stahlhütte »Rosta« als Ort des industriellen Fortschritts ist mit der Form einer aufwärts strebenden Spirale verschmolzen und geben der Politik der Kommunistischen Internationale Gestalt. Die Grundsatzdiskussion verlief also entlang der Frage, ob sich die revolutionäre Kunst in den Dienst einer gesellschaftlichen Wirklichkeit stellt, wodurch die Form mehr oder weniger willkürlich wäre, oder aber, ob die Kunst durch ihre Formen Inhalte selbst schafft, wobei nun »Wirklichkeit« in diesem Sinne als zunächst ungestaltetes Material aufzufassen wäre, der erst die Kunst ihre spezifische Sichtbarkeit zu geben vermag.

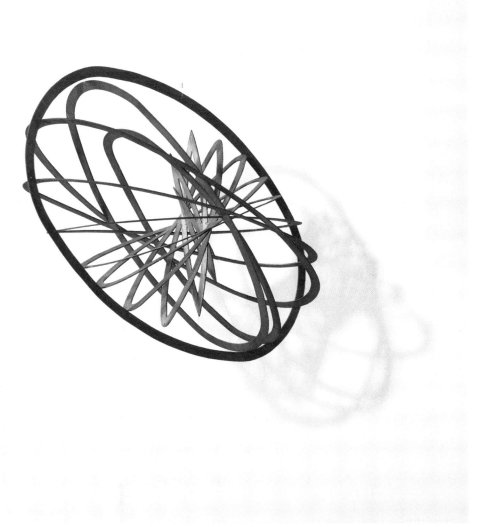

Spatial Construction No.12, Alexander Rodchenko, c.1920

Unbuildable Tatlin?!

not emerge from a perception that Tatlin's material culture contradicted Trotzky's formal manifesto, since the latter emphasizes in the chapter "Revolutionary Art and Socialist Art": "In accordance with the strong tendency of industrial culture we believe that artistic fantasy in the field of material goods production will deal with the design of the ideal object form as such and not with the ornament as an artistic free gift for the object itself."[4]

Instead Trotzky questioned Tatlin's use of a "glass bottle" (!) for an international world organization. For, as Pontus Hulten pointed out seventy years later, the experiences of the Cold War and Glasnost must, of course, be taken into consideration. "(Tatlin's) idea was quite clear and simple and—for me—extremely interesting: the idea that if you keep this power—which means the people who have that power—in constant movement, a certain uneasiness is generated so that they will also keep moving."[5] In retrospect, the monument for a Communist world organization suddenly develops into the model for a social utopia of a post-Communist era: "(The tower) is a romantic departure into a new classless civilization and expresses the overcoming of the ancient injustice of the division of peoples. It is the new, finally completed Tower of Babel. With Tatlin's tower emerges a new conception of a free humanity and the free, harmonious, human being."[6]

Completely free from a political reading of the aesthetics, Hubertus Gaßner sees an organic form in the curved line (of the spiral exterior frame), which is intrinsically given to the material. "Tatlin (...) claims that the curved arcs of lines derive from the stressed material. In the curvature or bow,

Dass diese ästhetischen Positionen in einem Kunststreit zutiefst politisch sind, wird aus den zeitgenössischen und späteren Kommentaren zur Funktionsweise des Denkmals deutlich. Leo Trotzki befindet in seinem 1923 publizierten Hauptwerk zur Literaturkritik *Literatur und Revolution* das Stahlgerüst für viel zu schwerfällig und das Denkmal für die Komintern als bloßen Tempel des Gerüstbaus. Für ihn ist selbstverständlich, dass Sitzungen des Komitees sicher nicht in einem Zylinder stattzufinden haben und schon gar nicht in einem, der sich dreht und aus Glas sei.[3] Dabei widerspräche Tatlins Materialkultur keinesfalls dem formalen Programm Trotzkis, da letzterer in dem Kapitel »Revolutionskunst und sozialistische Kunst« betont: »Ganz im Einklang mit der großen Tendenz der Industriekultur glauben wir, dass die künstlerische Phantasie auf dem Gebiet der Produktion der materiellen Güter sich mit der Aufstellung der idealen Form des Gegenstands als solchem befassen wird und nicht mit der Verzierung als künstlerischen Gratisbeilage zu dem Gegenstand selbst.«[4] Stattdessen fragt Trotzki nach dem Zweck einer Glasflasche (!) für eine internationale Weltorganisation. Eine Antwort auf diese Frage gibt Pontus Hulten 70 Jahre später – wobei die Erfahrungen mit dem Kalten Krieg und Glasnost mit berücksichtigt werden müssen: »(Tatlins) Idee war meiner Meinung nach sehr klar und einfach und – für mich – äußerst interessant: Die Idee nämlich, dass man, wenn man diese Macht – das heißt die Leute, die die Macht besitzen – in ständiger Bewegung hält, eine gewisse Unruhe erzeugt, so daß sie nicht erstarren könne.«[5] Unversehens wird in der Rückschau aus einem Denkmal für eine Kommunistische

Development of a Bottle in Space, Umberto Boccioni, 1913

The Tower of Babel, Pieter Brueghel the Elder, 1563, Kunsthistorisches Museum, Vienna

the interior condition of the material is made visible." This is also the reason why it cannot be understood as constructivist or as geometrical in form.[7] This contradiction to Constructivism, of course, works well. Constructivism is equated with the domination of straight lines and rectangular forms, while the "organic" is almost logically identified with curved lines and arched surfaces.

Nevertheless, it should be kept in mind in this so seemingly obvious distinction that one of the main works of Italian Futurism speaks a completely different language.

Umberto Boccioni's piece *Development of a Bottle in Space* from 1912 is an example of the design of an object, consisting of convex and concave surfaces, that rises up from its base into the form of a bottle. The larger, rounder, forms at the bottle's base develop a space with a constant degree of curvature, which is unlimited but according to Riemann finite space which was conceptually and mathematically composed in the "Technical Manifesto of Futurist Sculpture" (1912): "We must start from the central core of the object that we want to create to discover new laws and respectively the new forms which, invisibly but mathematically calculable, bind it to the outer and the inner artistic infinitum."[8] The constructed homology between mathematical laws and artistic production thus would also provide access to the curved line in Tatlin's monument design and no contradiction would arise between these forms, the straight lines that also define the framework, and the contained geometrical base bodies: pyramid, cone, cylinder, and hemisphere. Tatlin's demand, which is not necessarily limited to the material

Weltorganisation ein Modell für eine Sozialutopie der nach-kommunistischen Zeit: »(Der Turm) ist ein romantischer Aufbruch in eine neue klassenlose Zivilisation und die Überwindung der uralten Ungerechtigkeit der Völkerentzweiung, er ist der neue, endlich vollendete Babylonische Turm. Mit Tatlins Turm erscheint eine neue Vorstellung von der freien Menschheit und dem freien, harmonischen Menschen.«[6]

Gänzlich befreit von einer politischen Deutbarkeit der Ästhetik sieht Hubertus Gaßner in der gekrümmten Linie (des spiralförmigen Außengerüsts) eine organische Form, die dem Material intrinsisch gegeben sei. »Tatlin (…) behauptet, die gekrümmten Linienbogen erwüchsen aus dem in Spannung versetzten Material. In der Krümmung oder Wölbung trete die innere Verfassung des Materials in Erscheinung.« Deshalb könne man sie auch nicht konstruktivistisch und somit als geometrische Form verstehen.[7] Die Entgegensetzung zum Konstruktivismus funktioniert natürlich dort gut, wo dieser mit der Vorherrschaft der geraden Linie und der rechtwinkligen Form gleichgesetzt wird und dagegen »organisch« beinahe logisch mit der gekrümmten Linie und der gewölbten Fläche identifiziert wird. Nun sollte indes bei dieser so fraglos augenscheinlichen Gegenüberstellung bedacht werden, dass eines der Hauptwerke des italienischen Futurismus eine ganz andere Sprache spricht. Umberto Boccionis Arbeit »Entwicklung einer Flasche im Raum« von 1912 ist ein Beispiel für die Erzeugung eines Gegenstands aus konvexen und konkaven Flächen, der sich steil aus einem Sockel zur Form einer Flache empor schraubt. Mit den größeren, runderen Formen am Fuße der Flasche wird ein

sciences alone, is "to find the precondition for the form (in) the material itself."[9] What really was "material" to the artist can be interpreted in different ways and is a point that should be highlighted along with the fact that this versatility comes closest to the aesthetic and political culture in the historical period around 1919.

1   Nicolay Punin, *Kommunismus und Futurismus (Antwort auf V. Sklovskij)*, Kunst der Kommune, 1919, 17, 30.3, p.3 cited in Hubertus Gaßner, Eckhart Gillen (eds), *Zwischen Revolutionskunst und Sozialistischem Realismus. Dokumente und Kommentare. Kunstdebatten in der Sowjetunion von 1917 bis 1934*, Cologne, 1979, D14, p.56.
2   Vgl. Andréj B. Nakov, "Kunst und Revolution in Rußland: Ein Konflikt zwischen der 'reinen' Form und dem 'neuen Klassenbewußtsein'", in *Tendenzen der Zwanziger Jahre*, exhibition catalogue, Berlin, 1977, p.117.
    Viktor Shklovsky's article was further published in 1919 in "Kunst und Kommune".
3   Leo Trotzky, "Literature and Revolution" (German ed., Vienna 1924), in *Vladimir Tatlin*, exhibition catalogue, Stockholm, 1968, p.62.
4   Trotzky 1924, p.172.
5   Pontus Hulten, "Die Stockholmer Rekonstruktion des Denkmals der Dritten Internationale" in Jürgen Harten (ed.), *Vladimir Tatlin. Leben, Werk, Wirkung. Ein internationales Symposium*, Cologne, 1993, p.25.
6   Wassili Rakitin, "Tatlin und die Revolution" in Jürgen Harten (see note 4), p.250.
7   Hubertus Gaßner, "Auf der Suche nach Materialgerechtigkeit. Mißverständnisse und gekrümmte Linien" in Jürgen Harten (see note 4), p.42.
8   Cited by Margit Rowell, *Skulptur im 20. Jahrhundert: Figur, Raumkonstruktion, Prozeß*, Munich, 1986, p.265.
9   Gaßner (see note 6), p.43.

Raum mit konstantem Krümmungsmaß erzeugt, der unbegrenzt aber endlich im Sinne Riemannscher Flächen aufgefasst ist und der im *Technischen Manifest der futuristischen Bildhauerei* (1912) konzeptionell mathematisch gefasst wurde: »Wir müssen vom zentralen Kern des Gegenstands, den wir schaffen wollen, ausgehen, um die neuen Gesetze, d.h. die neuen Formen zu entdecken, die ihn unsichtbar aber mathematisch berechenbar an das äußere bildnerische Infinitum und an das innere bildnerische Infinitum binden.«[8] Die hergestellte Homologie von mathematischen Gesetzen und künstlerischer Produktion wäre also ebenfalls ein Zugang zur gekrümmten Linie in Tatlins Denkmalsentwurf und es entstünde kein Widerspruch zwischen diesen Formen, den ebenfalls das Gerüst definierenden Geraden und den geometrischen Grundkörpern darinnen: Pyramide, Kegel, Zylinder und Halbkugel. »(Im) Material selbst die Vorbedingung zur Form ausfindig zu machen«, mit dieser Forderung zitiert Gaßner Tatlin,[9] muss nicht notwendig auf die Werkstoffkunde allein bezogen sein. Was dem Künstler alles »Material« war, lässt sich vielseitig deuten, dies sollte aufgezeigt werden, und auch, dass diese Vielseitigkeit der ästhetischen und politischen Kultur der historischen Zeit um 1919 am nahesten kommt.

1   Nicolai Punin, *Kommunismus und Futurismus«* (Antwort auf V. Sklovskij), Kunst der Kommune, 1919, Nr. 17, 30.3., S. 3. Zitiert nach: Hubertus Gaßner, Eckhart Gillen (Hg.): *Zwischen Revolutionskunst und Sozialistischem Realismus. Dokumente und Kommentare. Kunstdebatten in der Sowjetunion von 1917 bis 1934*, Köln 1979, D14, S.56.
2   Vgl. Andréj B. Nakov, Kunst und Revolution in Rußland – Ein Konflikt zwischen der »reinen« Form und dem «neuen Klassenbewußtsein«. In: *Tendenzen der Zwanziger Jahre*, Ausstellungskatalog, Berlin 1977, S.117.

Wiktor Schklowskis Artikel erschien ebenfalls 1919
in *Kunst und Kommune.*

3   Leo Trotzki, »Literature and Revolution« (Deutsche
      Ausgabe, Wien 1924). In: *Vladimir Tatlin,*
      Ausstellungskatalog, Stockholm 1968, S.62.

4   Leo Trotzki, »Literatur und Revolution«,
      Wien 1924, S.172.

5   Pontus Hulten, »Die Stockholmer Rekonstruktion
      des Denkmals der Dritten Internationale«.
      In: Jürgen Harten (Hg.), *Vladimir Tatlin. Leben,*
      Werk, Wirkung. Ein internationales Symposium,
      Köln 1993, S.25.

6   Wassili Rakitin, »Tatlin und die Revolution«.
      In: Jürgen Harten (s. Anm. 4), S.250.

7   Hubertus Gaßner, »Auf der Suche nach Material-
      gerechtigkeit. Mißverständnisse und gekrümmte
      Linien«. In: Jürgen Harten (s. Anm. 4), S.42.

8   Zitiert nach Margit Rowell, *Skulptur im 20. Jahr-*
      hundert: Figur – Raumkonstruktion – Prozeß,
      München 1986, S.265.

9   Gaßner (s. Anm. 6), S. 43.

The ArcelorMittal Orbit by Anish Kapoor and Arup, Olympic Park, London, 2012

The Curved Line as Form, Metaphor, and Policy   75

The Theory of Spirals

Georg Glaeser

Spiralentheorie

Georg Glaeser

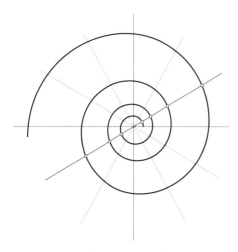

Figure 1: Logarithmic: exponential growth

Figure 2: Archimedean: linear growth

Spirals play an important role in nature, the arts, religions and—of course—in mathematics and geometry. An arbitrary planar spiral is drawn quickly on any sheet of paper or a wall of a cave. In Figure 1 and Figure 2, the most important classes of spirals are introduced in detail. Here follows a short summary of this classification:

PLANAR SPIRALS

In general, any curve in the plane that infinitely curls around a center C may be considered a spiral. Among them, two kinds play an important role in nature:

Logarithmic spiral (Fig.1)

To a mathematician, its polar equation (radius r, polar angle u) could both not be simpler and more aesthetic: r = au,

Spiralen spielen eine wichtige Rolle in der Natur, Kunst, Religion und – natürlich – der Mathematik und Geometrie. Eine einfache ebenflächige Spirale lässt sich leicht auf ein Blatt Papier oder die Wand einer Höhle malen. In Abbildung 1 und Abbildung 2, werden die wichtigsten Spiralformen detailliert angeführt. Hier geben wir nun eine kurze Zusammenfassung dieser Klassifikationen.

EBENFLÄCHIGE SPIRALEN

Generell kann jede Kurve, die sich in der Ebene unendlich um ein Zentrum Z dreht, als Spirale angesehen werden. Aus dieser Gruppe spielen zwei Formen eine wichtige Rolle in der Natur:

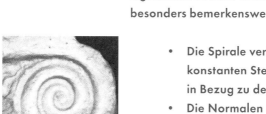

Antique column with spirals, logarithmic and Archimedean

where a is an arbitrary real number. a = 1 leads to the trivial solution, the unit circle. The following properties of such a spiral are quite remarkable:

- The spiral has a constant aviation angle with respect to the radial rays.
- The spiral's normals envelope another—congruent—logarithmic spiral.
- The curve has a self-similarity such that any part of it can be obtained by any other part by a simple magnification plus a rotation. Thus, the knowledge of one winding is sufficient for the knowledge of the whole curve.
- Although consisting of an infinite number of windings, the curve is not infinitely long and has a distinct arc length.

Logarithmische Spirale (Abb.1)

Für einen Mathematiker könnte ihre Polargleichung (Radius r, Polarwinkel u) nicht einfacher und zugleich ästhetischer sein: r = au, wobei a eine beliebige reelle Zahl darstellt. a = 1 führt zu der trivialsten Lösung, dem Einheitskreis. Die folgenden Eigenschaften einer solchen Spirale sind besonders bemerkenswert:

- Die Spirale verfügt über einen konstanten Steigungswinkel in Bezug zu den Radialstrahlen.
- Die Normalen einer Spirale umschließen eine weitere – kongruente – logarithmische Spirale.
- Die Kurve verfügt über Selbstähnlichkeit, so dass jeder Teil der Kurve durch eine einfache Vergrößerung und Rotation eines anderen Teils der Kurve bestimmt werden kann. Dadurch kann, selbst wenn nur eine Windung bekannt ist, die ganze Kurve bestimmt werden.
- Obwohl die Kurve aus einer unendlichen Anzahl von Windungen besteht, ist die Kurve doch nicht unendlich lang und verfügt über eine eindeutige Kreislänge.

Archimedische Spirale (Abb.2)

Ihre polare Gleichung (Radius r, Polarwinkel u) ist vergleichbar einfach: r = a × u, wobei a eine beliebige reelle Zahl darstellt. Und obwohl die Gleichung jener der logarithmischen Spirale ähnelt, verfügt diese Kurve doch über weniger bemerkenswerte Eigenschaften:

Archimedean spiral (Fig.2)

Its polar equation (radius r, polar angle u) is similarly simple:
$r = a \times u$, where a is an arbitrary real number. Even though the equation looks similar to the one of the logarithmic spiral, this curve has less remarkable properties:

- There is no more self-similarity. The curve consists of two congruent branches, divided by the center C.
- The radial distance of two neighboring windings is constant.

Other planar spiral

As we said, we could theoretically call any kind of wound-up planar curve a spiral. For instance, a projection of a helix produces spiral-like images. The helix itself is not included among the spirals (Fig.3).

- Es gibt keine Selbstähnlichkeit mehr. Die Kurve besteht aus zwei kongruenten Ästen, die durch das Zentrum Z geteilt werden.
- Der Radialabstand zweier benachbarter Windungen ist konstant.

Andere ebenflächige Spiralen

Wie bereits festgestellt, könnten wir theoretisch jede irgendwie gewundene ebenflächige Kurve als Spirale bezeichnen. Die Projektion einer Helix produziert z.B. spiralähnliche Bilder. Die Helix selbst wird jedoch nicht zu den Spiralen gezählt (Abb.3).

Eine weitere bemerkenswerte Spirale ist die Klothoide oder Eulersche Spirale, entlang derer die Krümmung proportional zur Kreislänge ist. Teile solcher Spiralen werden im Straßenbau verwendet (Abb.4).

Figure 3: A helix and not a spiral

Figure 4: Clothoid or double spiral

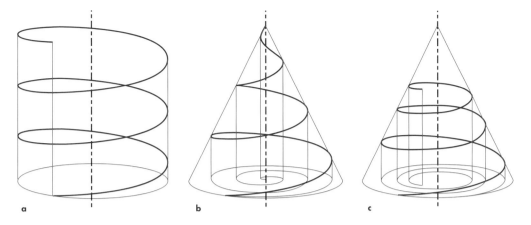

a   b   c

Three different types of space curves: a—Note that the helix is not considered as a spiral (top view = circle). b—Helispiral (top view = Archimedean spiral). c—Classic (cylindro-conic) spiral (top view = logarithmic spiral). Although Tatlin's spirals come close to the helispirals, they cannot be described by means of a formula.

Horns of a goat are helispiral surfaces.

Exponential natural growth — best seen in the shells of the Nautilus, mussels and snails.

One more remarkable spiral is called clothoid or Euler's spiral, the curvature of which is proportional to the arc length. Parts of such spirals are used in road construction (Fig.4).

SPIRALS IN SPACE

The two major types of planar spirals can be extended to 3D-space as follows. The radial rays are interpreted as the top view of the straight lines on an upright cone of revolution. Instead of rotating around the center C, we now rotate around the cylinder's axis. This leads to the corresponding curves:

Classic (cylindro-conic) spirals with logarithmic spirals as top view (Fig.5)

As to be expected, this first type inherits many outstanding geometrical properties. For instance, it has a constant slope with respect to the base plane and a constant aviation angle with respect to the generating line of the cone. Although winding infinitely (without ever reaching the apex of the cone), its arc length is again not infinite. In nature, such spirals are to be seen on snail-shells—as a result of exponential growth combined with a rotation.

Helispirals with Archimedean spirals as top view (Fig.6)

Though still remarkable, these curves have less impressing properties. Two neighboring windings, for instance, always have constant distance. Helispirals can also be found in nature, for instance on the horns of antilopes and buffalos. By the way: Tatlin's spirals closely resemble helispirals.

SPIRALEN IM RAUM

Die beiden Hauptformen ebenflächiger Spiralen können wie folgt in den dreidimensionalen Raum übertragen werden. Die Radialstrahlen werden als Draufsicht der geraden Linien eines aufrechten Drehkegels angesehen. Anstatt uns um das Zentrum Z zu drehen, drehen wir nun um die Zylinderachse. Das führt zu den folgenden Kurven:

Klassische (zylindrischkonische) Spirale mit logarithmischer Spirale als Draufsicht (Abb.5)

Wie zu erwarten übernimmt dieser erste Typ viele außergewöhnliche geometrische Eigenschaften. Sie verfügt z.B. über eine konstante Steigung in Bezug zur Grundebene und einen konstanten Steigungswinkel in Bezug zur Erzeugungslinie des Kegels. Und obwohl sie sich unendlich dreht (ohne dabei jemals den Scheitelpunkt des Kegels zu erreichen), ist ihre Kreislänge dennoch wieder nicht unendlich.

In der Natur kommen solche Spiralen auf Schneckenhäusern vor – als Resultat eines mit einer Drehung kombinierten exponentiellen Wachstums.

Helispiralen mit Archimedischen Spiralen als Draufsicht (Abb.6)

Obwohl sie noch immer bemerkenswert sind, verfügen diese Spiralen über weniger eindrucksvolle Eigenschaften. Zwei benachbarte Windungen haben z.B. immer einen konstanten Abstand. Auch Helispiralen kommen in der Natur vor, z.B. auf den Hörnern von Antilopen oder Büffeln Übrigens: Tatlins Spiralen kommen einer Helispirale am nächsten.

Spirals can also be created as orbits of points in space under the influence of geometrical transformations and/or physical forces. The classic spirals are the orbits of points in space that rotate around an axis and at the same time—proportionally to the rotation angle—change their distance to a fixed point on the axis (the cone's apex).

Very similarly, helispirals can be explained as orbits of points in space that not only rotate around an axis but move with proportional speed on the corresponding radial rays towards a fixed point on the axis. This leads to a third remarkable class of spatial spirals:

Spiralen können unter dem Einfluss geometrischer Transformationen und/oder physikalischer Kräfte auch als Kreisbahn von Punkten im Raum erzeugt werden. Klassische Spiralen sind die Kreisbahnen von Raumpunkten, die sich um eine Achse drehen und zur selben Zeit – proportional zum Rotationswinkel – ihren Abstand zu einem fixen Punkt der Achse (dem Kegelscheitelpunkt) verändern.

Sehr ähnlich können Helispiralen als Kreisbahnen von Raumpunkten erklärt werden, die sich nicht nur um eine Achse drehen, sondern sich auch auf den entsprechenden Radialstrahlen mit proportionaler Geschwindigkeit auf einen bestimmten Punkt der Achse zubewegen.

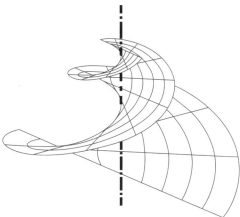

Figure 5: Classic spirals in space
(top view = logarithmic spirals)

Figure 6; Helispiral surface; top view:
Archimedean spirals

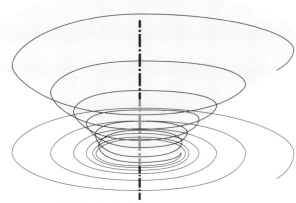

Figure 7: Galactic spiral

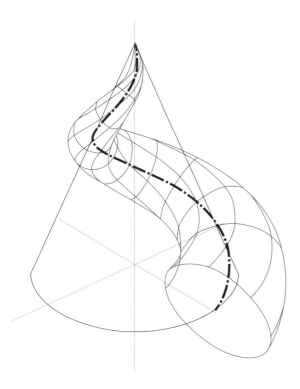

Figure 8; Linear natural growth — typically to be seen with animal horns.

Figure 9; View of a developable helispiral surface. Inspiration by nature — under the influence of currents, soft surfaces tend to have constant tangent planes along the generating lines and thus being developable.

Galactic spirals (Fig.7)

Galactic spirals are orbits of points rotating about an axis which are at the same time attracted by a gravitational force on the axis.[1] Most probably, such orbits are very frequent in universe. Their bearing surfaces are not cones but more general surfaces of revolution.

SPIRAL SURFACES

If not only points but entire generating curves are subject of a spiral motion, this leads to spiral surfaces. For instance, one can find such a generating curve for most of the shells, mussels and some cephalopods. The shell is then almost perfectly approximated by a classic spiral surface. This proves that the growth of such shells is exponential (Fig.2).

Helispiral surfaces occur, when growth is linear. Figure 8 illustrates that animal horns obviously grow linearly. As a last example, Figure 9 shall illustrate that spiral surfaces consisting of some soft material can adapt their properties.

1   G. Glaeser: *Geometrie und ihre Anwendungen in Kunst, Natur und Technik*, 2nd edition. Spektrum akademischer Verlag, Heidelberg 2006.

2   G. Glaeser: *Der mathematische Werkzeugkasten – Anwendungen in Natur und Technik*, 3rd edition. Spektrum akademischer Verlag, Heidelberg 2008.

Das führt uns zu einer bemerkenswerten dritten Form von Raumspiralen, den sogenannten:

Galaktischen Spiralen (Abb.7)

Galaktische Spiralen sind Kreisbahnen von Punkten, die sich um eine Achse drehen und gleichzeitig von einer Gravitationskraft auf der Achse angezogen werden.[1] Solche Kreisbahnen sind im Universum sehr wahrscheinlich. Ihre Tragoberflächen sind keine Kegel, sondern einfachere Drehflächen.

SPIRALOBERFLÄCHEN

Wenn nicht nur Punkte, sondern ganze Erzeugungskurven Gegenstand einer Spiralbewegung sind, führt dies zu Spiraloberflächen. Diese Erzeugungskurven können z.B. für die meisten Schalen, Muscheln und einige Kopffüßer gefunden werden.

Die Schalen nähern sich dann fast perfekt einer klassischen Spiraloberfläche an. Das beweist, dass das Wachstum solcher Schalen exponentiell ist.

Helispiraloberflächen entstehen, wenn das Wachstum linear ist. Abbildung 8 zeigt, dass Tierhörner offensichtlich linear wachsen.

Als letztes Beispiel soll Abbildung 9 demonstrieren, dass Spiraloberflächen aus weichem Material ihre Beschaffenheit anpassen können.

1   G. Glaeser: Geometrie und ihre Anwendungen in Kunst, Natur und Technik, 2. Auflage. Spektrum akademischer Verlag, Heidelberg 2006.

2   G. Glaeser: Der mathematische Werkzeugkasten – Anwendungen in Natur und Technik, 3. Auflage. Spektrum akademischer Verlag, Heidelberg 2008.

About the seminar

Zum Seminar

Unbuildable Tatlin?!

Klaus Bollinger, Wilfried Braumüller,
Florian Medicus, 2007

Unbuildable Tatlin?!

Klaus Bollinger, Wilfried Braumüller,
Florian Medicus, 2007

Model of the *Monument to the Third International*, Petrograd, 1920

While making our first preparations for the seminar "Unbuildable Tatlin?!" we already had to acknowledge the presence of the *Monument to the Third International* in contemporary architecture and arts and that disputes about it were as diverse as they were strange. Until today and—as we can safely assume—for many more years to come, Tatlin's design enthralls and occupies artists, literary men and scientists worldwide. Vladimir Tatlin's monument stands symbolically for the most thrilling, diverse and far many decades influential trend in the arts of the 20th century both as a symbol and a turning point. It lifts itself high above all the other fantastic designs, products and ideas of the so-called Russian avant-garde for the simple fact that already ninety years ago it divided history into a before and after. There was simply no way around Tatlin's tower. And this is not only due to its originally planned height of 400 meters but also to the way in which Tatlin and his coworkers designed this ultimately political propaganda machine, and how they specified it and how geometries, volumes and constructions produced a completely new standard and coherence. All of this together still impresses and challenges us equally today just as it did ninety years ago.

At the beginning of the seminar we tried to find out during the course entitled *Supporting Structures* 3 if anybody before us had already studied in detail the original construction and the ensuing static problems. Is the monument which is deemed "unbuildable" in principle constructible? Should the construction of the models be enhanced and which effects would that have on the original design

Schon bei den Vorbereitungen des Seminars »Unbuildable Tatlin?!« war uns aufgefallen, wie hartnäckig sich das Monument zur III. Internationalen in der zeitgenössischen Architektur- und Kunstlandschaft behauptet. Die Auseinandersetzungen sind so vielfältig wie kurios. Bis heute, und – wie man ruhig annehmen darf – noch viele Jahre, begeistert und beschäftigt Tatlins Entwurf Kunstschaffende, Literaten und Wissenschaftler weltweit. Wladimir Tatlins Monument steht vor allem sinnbildlich für eine der wohl spannendsten, vielfältigsten und über die Jahrzehnte prägendsten Kunstströmungen des 20. Jahrhunderts, als Symbol und Wendepunkt. Aus den vielen phantastischen Entwürfen, Produkten und Ideen der so genannten russischen Avantgarde aber hebt sich das Monument entschieden ab; teilte es doch schon vor fast 90 Jahren die Geschichte in ein *Davor* und *Danach*; an Tatlins Turm konnte keiner vorbei. Das aber lag gewiss nicht ausschließlich an der ursprünglich geplanten Höhe von 400 Metern; die Art wie Tatlin und seine Mitarbeiter eine letztlich politische Propagandamaschine gedanklich entwarfen, sie funktional durchdetaillierten, wie Geometrien, Volumina und Konstruktionen einen vollkommen neuen Anspruch und Zusammenhalt erfuhren, das alles zusammen beeindruckt und fordert uns heute gleichsam heraus.

Wir haben zu Beginn des Seminars im Rahmen der *Tragkonstruktionen* 3 versucht in Erfahrung zu bringen, ob sich schon vor uns jemand eingehend mit der eigentlichen Konstruktion und den statischen Schwierigkeiten auseinandergesetzt hat. Wäre das als »unbaubar« geltende Monument nicht doch baubar? Müsste man

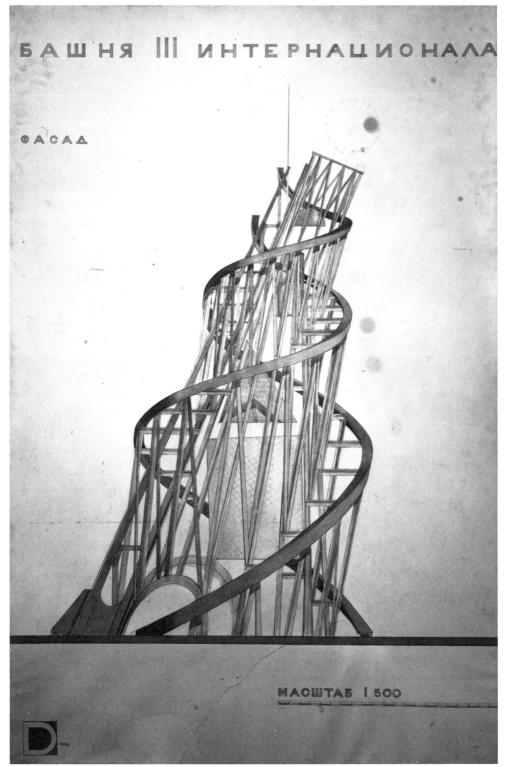

БАШНЯ III ИНТЕРНАЦИОНАЛА

ФАСАД

МАСШТАБ 1 500

Section of the *Monument to the Third International*, Vladimir Tatlin

БАШНЯ III ИНТЕРНАЦИОНАЛА

РАЗРЕЗ ПО I-I

МАСШТАБ I 500

Section of the *Monument to the Third International*, Vladimir Tatlin

approach? Could we build the tower today or could it have been built 90 years ago? It was and still is our goal to perform a thoroughly constructional analysis of Tatlin's *Monument to the Third International* and thus deliver proof for its constructability at the original scale. This—and so much may be said in advance—was achieved by the students.

It fits Vladimir Yevgrafovich Tatlin's biography that almost no documents regarding his most famous project have survived (it is rumored that he destroyed many of his own works on purpose for the simple reason that Kasimir Malevich was not supposed to examine and copy them). Two concept drawings from 1919 exist, two photos depicting work on the model (1920, with his coworkers T. Shapiro, I. Meyerzon and P. Vinogradov) as well as some photos of the finished model in St. Petersburg and later in Moscow. These documents were the basis of our research. The tower's third and final version was exhibited at the Soviet Pavilion in Paris in 1925, in which Tatlin had strongly reduced the vertical elements to increase the spiral's dynamic. This model was unfortunately lost and the photos are not very helpful. Thus we had to orient ourselves on the model of 1920.

The model from 1920 was constructed without any further planning or model tests and was only based on the two above mentioned drawings. In contrast to the drawings, construction seems to have been expanded and further enhanced in many areas. To be able to emulate this process we asked the students to form two groups after an initial study of the art-historical circumstances. One group

die Konstruktion der Modelle verbessern, und wenn ja, welche Auswirkungen hätte das auf den ursprünglichen Entwurfsansatz? Wäre der Turm heute baubar oder: schon vor 90 Jahren baubar gewesen?

Ziel war und ist es nach wie vor, Tatlins Monument zur III. Internationalen einer gründlichen konstruktiven Analyse zu unterziehen und den Nachweis der Baubarkeit im ursprünglichen Maßstab zu erbringen; das – und so weit wollen wir vorgreifen – ist den Studierenden gelungen.

Es passt zur Biografie von Wladimir Evgrafovič Tatlin, dass von seinem wohl bekanntesten Projekt kaum Unterlagen vorhanden sind (man sagt, er habe mehrere seiner Arbeiten vorsätzlich zerstört, nur dass Kasimir Malewitsch sie nicht sehen und kopieren konnte). Es gibt lediglich die zwei Entwurfszeichnungen aus dem Jahr 1919, zwei Fotografien von der Arbeit am Modell (1920, mit seinen Mitarbeitern T. Schapiro, I. Meierson und P. Winogradow), sowie einige Fotografien des fertigen Modells in St. Petersburg und später in Moskau. Diese Unterlagen bildeten jedenfalls die Basis unserer Untersuchung. Die dritte und letzte Version des Turms wurde 1925 in Paris im Pavillon der Sowjetunion ausgestellt. Tatlin hatte die vertikalen Elemente stark reduziert, um die Dynamik der Spirale noch zu verstärken. Dieses Modell ist leider verschollen und die Fotografien zu wenig aussagekräftig. So mussten wir uns am Stand des Jahres 1920 orientieren.

Das Modell von 1920 wurde ohne weitere Planungen oder Modellversuche nur aufgrund der zwei oben erwähnten Zeichnungen errichtet. Der Aufbau scheint gegenüber den Zeichnungen konstruktiv ausgebaut und in vielen Bereichen

was to build a 3D-model based only on the drawings and expand the thus collected raw data in a logical constructive way, which in the end should not or did not have to necessarily mirror the model's picture. The other group was to rectify the tower's old photos with the help of the Chair of Geometry (see p.95) and thus to get as authentic data as possible for further processing.

Parallel to that the students tried to compose a short history of the construction from 1870 to 1920. The achievements from that period are to a large degree still remarkably up to date even today. This is not only true for constructional steelwork but in general for the powerful and optimistic structural ideas and designs. In 1914 Tatlin had visited Paris and of course seen the Eiffel Tower, while in his home country Karl Joganson was developing the first Tensegrity structures and a certain Vladimir Shukhov had started the construction of material-saving, hyperbolical steel lattice formwork towers. It may seem a bit ironical that Shukhov was contracted with building a tower the same year as Tatlin. The radio tower of the Comintern radio station Schabolovka in Moscow with a height of 350 meters would only have needed one quarter of the amount of steel needed for the construction of the Eiffel Tower standing at 300 meters (build in 1889). Due to the fact that there were no 2200 tons of building steel available in Moscow at that time, Lenin instead decided on a version of 150 meters, which can still be visited today.

The next steps in the seminar were the comparison of the 3D-models with the constructional optimization. This was made possible thanks to the support of

verbessert worden zu sein. Um diesen Prozess nachempfinden zu können, ersuchten wir die Studierenden sich nach einem ersten Abtasten der kunstgeschichtlichen Umstände in zwei Gruppen zu teilen. Eine Gruppe sollte nur aufgrund der Zeichnungen ein 3D-Modell erstellen und diese Rohdaten in logisch-konstruktiver Hinsicht ausbauen, was nicht unbedingt dem Bild des Turms entsprechen sollte oder musste.

Die andere Gruppe durfte sich mithilfe des Ordinariats für Geometrie (siehe S.95) daran machen, die alten Fotografien des Modells zu entzerren, um möglichst authentische Daten zur Weiterbearbeitung zu erhalten.

Parallel dazu wurde seitens der Studierenden versucht, eine kleine Geschichte der Konstruktion in den Jahren 1870 bis 1920 zusammenzustellen. Die Errungenschaften aus dieser Epoche sind großteils noch heute bemerkenswert aktuell. Das betrifft nicht nur den konstruktiven Stahlbau, sondern im Allgemeinen die kraftvollen und optimistischen strukturellen Ideen und Entwürfe. Tatlin hatte 1914 Paris besucht und natürlich den Eiffelturm gesehen, während in seiner Heimat Karl Joganson erste Tensegrity-Strukturen entwickelte und sich ein gewisser Wladimir Šuchov daran machte, materialsparende, hyperbolische Stahlfachwerktürme zu konstruieren. Es mag eine gewisse Ironie dahinter liegen, dass Šuchov im selben Jahr wie Tatlin mit dem Bau eines Turms beauftragt wurde. Der Sendeturm der Komintern-Radiostation Schabolovka in Moskau hätte bei einer Höhe von 350 Metern nur ein Viertel der Stahlmenge des 300 Meter hohen Eiffelturms (gebaut 1889) verbraucht. Da aber zu dieser Zeit in Moskau keine 2200 Tonnen

The engineer Kurt Polanec in a practical program calculating of spatial frameworks. After various attempts the primary construction was able to support its own weight. The monument's inner rotating volumes remain unexplained for the moment since even Tatlin did not provide any con-structional statements for them. At the Moscow exhibition a small boy was sitting at the base operating a transmission system with a crank handle and the volumes were made of paper marked with a net-work of lines to represent a steel and glass construction.

During the course of the seminar further optimization runs proved necessary to transfer the expected loads from the inner volumes to the primary structure. Now the final step is to demonstrate that the volumes can be rotated according to Tatlin's design. This, however, would have gone beyond the scope of our seminar, which we hope was a rewarding experience for all participants.

Now that the constructability of the *Monument to the Third International* has been proven, we join Ilja Ehrenburg in asking, "Where can we get the steel and other metal for realization so that the model can become a monument?"[1]

1   Ilja Ehrenburg 'E pur se muove', Berlin, 1922; *Wladimir Tatlin 1885–1953*, Kunstverein München, 1970

Baustahl verfügbar waren, verfolgte Lenin eine 150 Meter hohe Version, die man noch heute in Moskau besuchen kann.

Die nächsten Schritte in unserem Seminar waren die Vergleiche der 3D-Modelle und die konstruktive Optimie-rung. Dies geschah, mit dankenswerter Unterstützung von Dipl.Ing. Kurt Polanec in einem praxisnahen Berechnungsprogramm für räumliche Stabwerke. Nach mehreren Versuchen »stand« die Primärstruktur unter Eigenlast. Ungeklärt blieben vorerst jedoch die sich drehenden Volumina im Inneren des Monuments. Hierzu gibt es auch von Tatlin keine konstruktiven Aussagen. Bei der Moskauer Ausstellung saß ein kleiner Junge unter dem Sockel und betätigte ein Übersetzungssystem mit einer Handkurbel, die Körper waren aus Papier und sollten mit ihren aufgemalten Liniennetzen eine Stahl-Glas-Konstruktion darstellen.

Es waren im weiteren Verlauf des Seminars noch einige Optimierungsdurch-läufe notwendig um die zu erwartenden Lasten aus den inneren Körpern auf die Pri-märstruktur zu übertragen. Es bliebe jetzt noch nachzuweisen, dass sich die Volumina auch entsprechend Tatlins Vorstellungen bewegen ließen. Das aber ging über den Rahmen unserer Lehrveranstaltung, hinaus die allen Beteiligten viel Interessantes näher gebracht und zudem viel Freude bereitet hat.

Jetzt, wo die Baubarkeit des Monu-ments zur III. Internationalen nachgewiesen wäre, schließen wir uns der Frage von Ilja Ehrenburg an: »Wo können wir das Eisen und das andere Metall für die Realisierung finden, so dass aus dem Modell ein Monu-ment werden kann?«[1]

1   Ilja Ehrenburg, in »E pur se muove«, Berlin, 1922; *Wladimir Tatlin 1885–1953*, Katalog Kunstverein München, 1970

Gustave Eiffel on the construction site of the Eiffel tower, July 18th, 1887, Louis-Emile Durandelle, Paris Musée d'Orsay

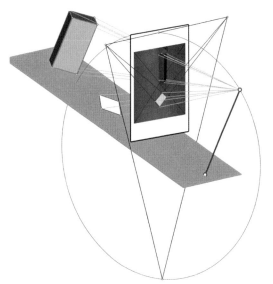

Figure 1: *Measuring point method*

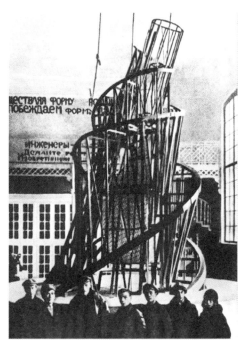

Figure 2: Photos with the same (right-hand) window corner

Geometric Reconstruction with Poor-Quality Photos

Franz Gruber

Geometrische Rekonstruktion basierend auf Fotos schlechter Bildqualität

Franz Gruber

Only a few poor quality photos of a scaled down model were available, making it difficult to analyze the 3D-geometry. These photos did not satisfy the conditions of current geometrical reconstruction methods. In addition to this problem, we also had to expect major inaccuracies in determining vanishing points. We are presenting a numerical method for reconstruction, which uses multiple photos (views) of one and the same object and minimizes the existing aberration with a stochastic algorithm.

DESCRIPTION OF THE PROBLEM

Since we had no plans of the building, our reconstruction was based on about ten, quite old photos (M1:100) of a scaled down model. By means of classic geometric methods that use principal vanishing points have been partially outdated by newer

Zur Bestimmung der 3D-Geometrie des Turms standen nur einige Fotos schlechter Bildqualität eines verkleinerten Modells zur Verfügung, welche leider nicht den Anforderungen geometrischer Rekonstruktionsmethoden entsprachen. Zusätzlich zu der schlechten Bildqualität mussten wir von groben Ungenauigkeiten in der Bestimmung der Fluchtpunkte ausgehen. Wir präsentieren eine numerische Rekonstruktionsmethode, die auf unterschiedlichen Fotos (Ansichten) desselben Objekts basiert und vorhandene Abweichungen mithilfe eines stochastischen Algorithmus minimiert.

PROBLEMBESCHREIBUNG

Da uns keine Pläne des Gebäudes zur Verfügung standen, basierte unsere Rekonstruktion auf rund zehn sehr alten Fotos (M1:100) eines verkleinerten Modells.

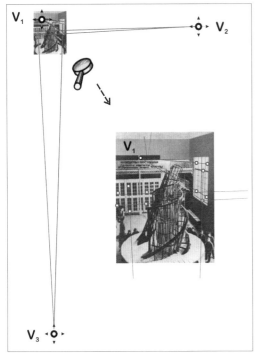

Figure 3: Vanishing point V₃ is far outside the image

Figure 4: Missing base point P' and the absolute reference system

numerical methods,[6,7] they are more appropriate for developing an algorithm for this special case. Our method is basically derived from the classical Measuring point method,[1,3,4,8] which only requires one adequate (ideal) photo for reconstruction.

First, this requires knowledge of the principal vanishing points (*Problem A*). Second, the vertical projection P' onto the ground (base point, see Fig. 4) of any reconstruction point P has to be apparent in the photo (*Problem B*).

     In our case, the vanishing points could be roughly estimated, while the vertical projections of the reconstruction points could not be determined reasonably from

Und obwohl einige der klassischen geometrischen Methoden, die Hauptflucht-punkte verwenden, aufgrund neuerer numerischer Methoden überholt sind,[6,7] sind sie in diesem speziellen Fall doch besser geeignet, einen Algorithmus zu entwickeln. Unsere Methode ist im Prinzip aus dem klassischen *Messpunktverfahren*[1,3,4,8] entwickelt, welches nur ein angemessenes (ideales) Foto zur Rekonstruktion benötigt.

Dafür müssen die Hauptfluchtpunkte genau bekannt sein (*Problem A*). Außerdem muss die vertikale Projektion P' auf die Grund-fläche (Basispunkt, siehe Abb. 4) jedes Rekonstruktionspunktes P auf dem Foto sichtbar sein (*Problem B*).

the photos. To solve this problem, we had to use at least two photos showing the same orthogonal reference system, for example, a table or the corner of a room. We were able to find exactly two photos of Tatlin's model with these properties. They depict the same window on the right-hand side, where the window corner served as our common reference system (Fig.2, 4). For some reason, the left picture has obviously been retouched in the background but, fortunately, this resulted in no further complications.

PROBLEM A: THE IMPRECISION OF THE VANISHING POINTS V_1, V_2, AND V_3

As a basic requirement, the classical reconstruction method needs the accurate positions of the vanishing points to obtain a satisfactory result. The positions of the vanishing points determine the position of the "Augpunkt" (point of view or "eye point") and also the position of the projection rays passing through the "eye point". Therefore, any inaccuracy in the vanishing points results in a propagated error during all calculations of the reconstruction.

Due to its large distance from the principal point, the vanishing point corresponding to the z-direction V_3 had the biggest domain of uncertainty (Fig.3). To solve the problem of the vanishing points, we roughly estimated their initial positions and varied them stochastically within their domain of uncertainty. This iterative series of vanishing points $(V_1, V_2, V_3)_i$ yields a series of hypothetical eye points, which formed the basis of our algorithm.

In unserem Fall konnten die Fluchtpunkte ungefähr bestimmt werden, während dies für die vertikalen Projektionen der Rekonstruktionspunkte auf dem Bild nicht möglich war. Um dieses Problem zu lösen, mussten wir mindestens zwei Fotos verwenden, die dasselbe orthogonale Bezugssystem aufwiesen, z.B. einen Tisch oder die Ecke eines Raumes. Wir fanden genau zwei Fotos von Tatlins Modell, die diese Eigenheiten aufwiesen. Sie zeigen dasselbe Fenster auf der rechten Seite, sodass das Fenster als gemeinsames Bezugssystem genutzt werden konnte (Abb. 2, 4).

Aus irgendeinem Grund war der Hintergrund des linken Bildes offenbar retuschiert worden, was jedoch glücklicherweise keine weiteren Probleme verursachte.

PROBLEM A: DIE UNGENAUIGKEIT DER FLUCHTPUNKTE V_1, V_2, V_3

Um mit der klassischen Rekonstruktionsmethode zu einem zufriedenstellenden Resultat zu gelangen braucht man die genauen Positionen der Fluchtpunkte. Diese Positionen bestimmen die Position des Blickwinkels (»Augpunkt«) und infolgedessen auch die Position der Projektionsstrahlen, die durch den Augpunkt laufen. Daher ergibt jede Ungenauigkeit der Fluchtpunkte einen Folgefehler in allen weiteren Berechnungen der Konstruktion.

Der Fluchtpunkt welcher der z-Richtung V_3 zugeordnet ist, wies aufgrund der weiten Entfernung zum Hauptpunkt den größten Unsicherheitsbereich auf (Abb.3). Um das Problem der Fluchtpunkte zu lösen, ermittelten wir ihre ungefähre ursprüngliche Position und variierten sie dann stochastisch

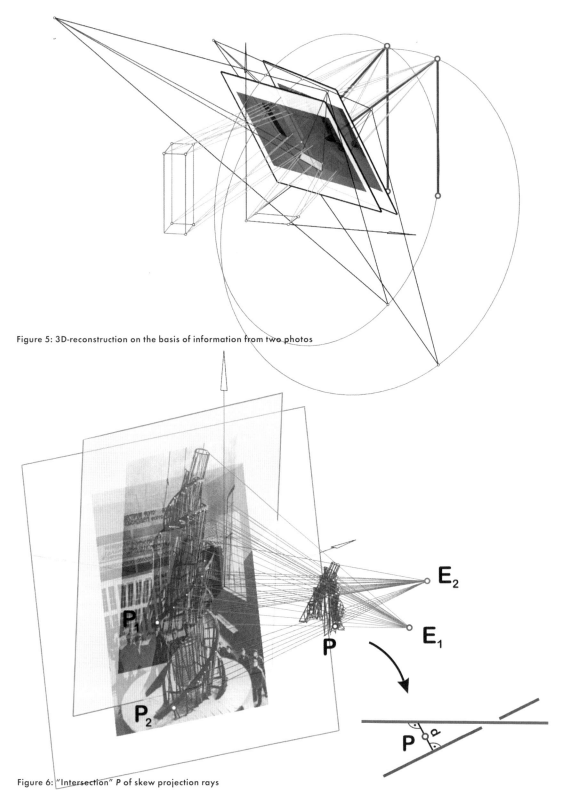

Figure 5: 3D-reconstruction on the basis of information from two photos

Figure 6: "Intersection" P of skew projection rays

PROBLEM B: MISSING BASE POINT P'

Since the base point P' (Fig. 4) was missing on the photo, we could not reconstruct the 3D-data of P from a single photo, as the Measuring point method suggests.[1,4,8] Nevertheless our approach is based on this classical method, modified to use the information of multiple photos of the same object. First, let us consider the case of a single photo. The initial estimated vanishing points $(V_1, V_2, V_3)_0$ correspond to the spatial directions $\{\vec{x}, \vec{y}, \vec{z}\}$ through a definite "point of view" E. The window corner O can be chosen as an absolute reference system and the whole scene can be transformed into this system.

In order to integrate the remaining photos, we transformed them all (together with their several "points of view") into the absolute reference system and scaled them to a common measuring unit (Fig. 5). Having done so, we were able to start with the reconstruction of the single point P, the 3D- coordinates of which originate from the intersection of two corresponding projection rays (belonging to different photos). Thus, we were able to work without the knowledge of the missing base point P'.

THE ALGORITHM AS A PROBLEM OF MINIMIZATION

The theoretical assumption that the corresponding projection rays are intersecting lines is impossible in practical terms, but nonetheless serves as the basic idea for the following algorithm. In practice, two corresponding projection rays E_1P_1 and E_2P_2 are skewed (Fig. 6) with a certain

in ihrem jeweiligen Unsicherheitsbereich. Diese iterative Reihe von Fluchtpunkten $(V_1, V_2, V_3)_i$ lieferte eine Reihe hypothetischer Augpunkte, welche die Grundlage unseres Algorithmus bildeten.

PROBLEM B: DER FEHLENDE BASISPUNKT P'

Aufgrund des fehlenden Basispunktes P' (Abb. 4) auf dem Foto konnten wir die 3D-Daten von P nicht wie im Messpunktverfahren vorgesehen[1,4,8] anhand eines einzelnen Fotos bestimmen. Trotzdem stützt sich unsere Vorgehensweise auf dieser klassischen Methode, jedoch dahingehend modifiziert, dass Informationen von mehreren verschiedenen Fotos desselben Objekts verwendet werden. Gehen wir einmal von einem einzelnen Foto aus. Die ursprünglich geschätzten Fluchtpunkte $(V_1, V_2, V_3)_0$ sind den räumlichen Richtungen $\{\vec{x}, \vec{y}, \vec{z}\}$ durch einen fixen Augpunkt E zugeordnet. Die Fensterecke O kann als absolutes Bezugssystem herangezogen werden, wodurch die ganze Ansicht in dieses System übertragen werden kann. Um die verbleibenden Fotos zu integrieren, wandeln wir sie alle (zusammen mit ihren jeweiligen Augpunkten) in das absolute Bezugssystem um und skalieren sie nach einer gemeinsamen Maßeinheit (Abb. 5).

Anschließend können wir mit der Rekonstruktion einzelner Punkte P beginnen, deren 3D-Koordinaten sich aus dem Schnittpunkt zweier zugeordneter Projektionsstrahlen (aus verschiedenen Fotos) ergeben. Dadurch können wir ohne die Daten des fehlenden Basispunktes P' arbeiten.

orthogonal distance $d > 0$. Let S be the sum of all those squared distances d_i^2 ($i = 1...n$, where n is the number of marked points in each photo). In our special case of using two photos, the algorithm has to minimize the functional S by stochastic variation of 6 vanishing points (see Problem A) with the ideal solution $S = 0$.

$$0 \leq S = \sum_{i=1}^{n} d_i^2 \rightarrow min\ (V_1, V_2, V_3)$$

Since any vanishing point has two degrees of freedom, we get a twelve-dimensional region $X \subset R_{12}$ for a non-linear minimization problem. This was the crucial factor in implementing a stochastic method,[2,5] instead of another numerical method.

QUALITY OF THE ALGORITHM

The algorithm described above converged amazingly well, which means that the sum of errors S had an exactly determinable minimum. The vanishing points and the accordant eye point in the minimum situation provide the optimal 3D-positions (Fig.6) of the reconstruction points. Later comparison with a model created by a group of students, using their visual intuition solely, yielded a high agreement with our numerical solution.

1   Richard Hartley and Andrew Zissermann, *Multiple View Geometry*, Cambridge: Cambridge University Press, 2000; Hellmuth Stachel, "Descriptive geometry meets computer vision: the geometry of two images," *Journal for Geometry and Graphics*, 10(2):137–153, 2006.
2   Heinrich Brauner, *Lehrbuch der Konstruktiven Geometrie*, Vienna and New York: Springer, 1986; Georg Glaeser, *Ein Beitrag zur Perspektive mit gekippter Grundebene*, 1994; Georg Glaeser, *Geometrie und ihre Anwendungen in Kunst, Natur und Technik*: Elsevier Spektrum Akademischer

DER ALGORITHMUS ALS PROBLEM DER MINIMIERUNG

Die theoretische Annahme, dass die zugeordneten Projektionsstrahlen sich schneidende Linien sind, ist praktisch unmöglich, aber die grundlegende Idee des folgenden Algorithmus. Praktisch verlaufen zwei zugeordnete Projektionsstrahlen E_1P_1 und E_2P_2 schief zueinander (Abb.6) mit einem bestimmten orthogonalen Abstand $d > 0$.

S sei hierbei die Summe all dieser quadrierten Abstände d_i^2 ($i = 1...n$, wobei n die Anzahl der markierten Punkte jedes Fotos darstellt). In unserem speziellen Fall mit zwei Fotos muss der Algorithmus das funktionale S durch stochastische Variation der 6 verschiedenen Fluchtpunkte minimieren (siehe Problem A), um die ideale Lösung $S = 0$ zu erreichen.

$$0 \leq S = \sum_{i=1}^{n} d_i^2 \rightarrow min\ (V_1, V_2, V_3)$$

Da jeder Fluchtpunkt über zwei Freiheitsgrade verfügt, erhalten wir einen zwölf-dimensionalen Bereich $X \subset R_{12}$ für ein nichtlineares Minimierungsproblem. Dies war der ausschlaggebende Faktor eine stochastische Methode[2,5] anstelle einer numerischen einzusetzen.

QUALITÄT DES ALGORITHMUS

Der oben beschriebene Algorithmus näherte sich erstaunlich gut an, was bedeutet, dass die Summe an Fehlern für S ein sehr genau bestimmbares Minimum aufwies.

Die Fluchtpunkte und der entsprechende Augpunkt in der Minimalsituation ergeben die optimalen 3D-Positionen

Verlag, 2005; Walter Wunderlich, *Darstellende Geometrie 2*, BI Hochschultaschenbücher 133/133a, Mannheim, 1967.

3   Brauner, 1986; Glaeser, 2005; Wunderlich, 1967.

4   S.M. Ermakov, *Die Monte-Carlo-Methode und verwandte Fragen*, Munich and Vienna: Oldenbourg, 1975; J.M. Hammersley and D.C. Handscomb, *Monte Carlo Methods: Monographs on Applied Probability and Statistics*: Chapman and Hall, 1979.

(Abb.6) der Rekonstruktionspunkte. Der spätere Vergleich mit einem von Studenten gebauten Modell, die sich beim Bau nur auf ihre visuellen Fähigkeiten verlassen haben, hat eine hohe Übereinstimmung mit unserer rechnerischen Lösung ergeben.

1   Heinrich Brauner. *Lehrbuch der Konstruktiven Geometrie*. SpringerWienNewYork, 1986.

2   S.M. Ermakov. *Die Monte-Carlo-Methode und verwandte Fragen*. Oldenbourg, München Wien, 1975.

3   Georg Glaeser. *Ein Beitrag zur Perspektive mit gekippter Grundebene*. 1994.

4   Georg Glaeser. *Geometrie und ihre Anwendungen in Kunst, Natur und Technik*. Elsevier Spektrum Akademischer Verlag, 2005.

5   J.M. Hammersley and D.C. Handscomb. *Monte Carlo Methods. Monographs on Applied Probability and Statistics*. Chapman and Hall, 1979.

6   Richard Hartley and Andrew Zissermann. *Multiple view geomerty*. Cambridge University Press, 2000.

7   Hellmuth Stachel. Descriptive geometry meets computer vision – the geometry of two images. *Journal for Geometry and Graphics*, 10(2):137–153, 2006.

8   Walter Wunderlich. *Darstellende Geometrie 2*, BI Hochschultaschenbücher 133/133a, Mannheim, 1967.

About the Seminar "Unbuildable Tatlin?!"

Florian Medicus, Kurt Polanec, 2009

Zum Seminar »Unbuildable Tatlin?!«

Florian Medicus, Kurt Polanec, 2009

The possibility of constructing Vladimir Tatlin's *Monument to the Third International* was already highly contested during the time of its production. A majority neverthe-less thought that the tower could actually be built, an assumption that has been mytholo-gized throughout the history of 20th century architecture. One goal of the "Unbuildable Tatlin" seminar was thus to examine whether the primary structure could have been built according to its optical specifications and whether it could have been realized with few restrictions in 1920. To cut a long story short, the answer is yes. The structure can be built in its original scale with some minor optical adaptations and optimizations, a fact that was proven by the students during the seminar.

Nevertheless, one major restriction had to be made. The freely hanging and rotating volumes inside the tower could not

Die tatsächliche Konstruktion von Wladimir Tatlins Monument zur III. Internationalen war schon zur Zeit seines Entstehens Grund für heftige Auseinandersetzungen. Mehr-heitlich hielt man den Turm damals aller-dings für baubar – ein Umstand, der sich als zweifelhaft-konstruktiver Mythos durch die Architekturgeschichte des 20. Jahr-hunderts aufrecht hielt. Ziel des Seminars »Unbuildable Tatlin?!« war es demnach, zu untersuchen, ob die Primärstruktur an sich, unter Miteinbeziehung der optischen Vorgaben baubar gewesen wäre und ob der Turm an sich 1920 (mit den Mitteln und Möglichkeiten seiner Zeit) überhaupt hätte gelingen können.

Um die wesentlichste Antwort vorwegzunehmen: ja, die Struktur ist mit optisch unwesentlichen Adaptionen bzw. Optimierungen im ursprünglichen Maßstab baubar; diesen Nachweis konnten die

Students

Tim Altenhof
Elena Berecova
Alexandre d'Aram
Alexander Diem
Sebastian Fischbeck
Sophie Grell
Thomas Hindelang
Andrea König
Benjamin Parbs
Daniel Podmirseg
Klaus Seits
Florian von Hayek
Anna Weilhartner

Tutors

Klaus Bollinger
Wilfried Braumüller
Florian Medicus
Georg Glaeser
Franz Gruber
Franz Hnizdo

Geometric interaction (seminar)

Geometric approximation (seminar)

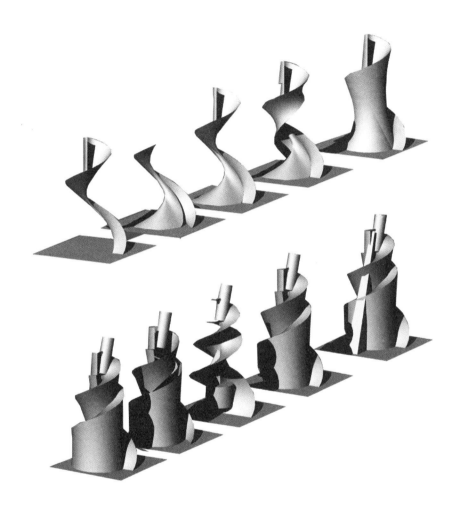

Geometric approximation, 3D (seminar)

Structural view, interior (seminar)

be worked into our static model during the course of the seminar and were thus substituted by so-called "unstrained members."

For the results from the calculation program RTSAB presented on the following pages, it was important to recreate the optical characteristics and basic proportions from Tatlin's model photos. The calculated results also only refer to the load from the structure's own weight—the material used for the whole structure is steel (ST52), with the weight of the statically effective members at 116 400 tonnes. An additional 10% was added for the node connections, which resulted in a final total weight of 128 000 tons. Thus if we take the often cited optical-constructive comparison between Tatlin's tower and the Eiffel Tower, which is 100 meters smaller, we could say that for every one of Tatlin's towers, thirteen Eiffel Towers could have been built. But neither Tatlin nor the students in the seminar saw this as a restriction.

Another remarkable feature of the strut-and-tie model is the enhanced deformation of the structure due to its asymmetrical construction and the irregular bearing pressures in the area of the "backbone." We can, for example, measure a (maximum) value of 200 000 kN bearing pressure at one point, but only 60 000 kN at the point diagonally opposite. These different values, very close to each other, would have created problems especially in the swampy ground of Saint Petersburg and would (even from a modern point of view) prompt a rethinking of the whole construction regardless of its visionary enthusiasm.

The problem of materials, such as that encountered in Vladimir Shukhov's tower in Moscow with its delightfully

StudentInnen in unserem Seminar erbringen. Wenngleich auch mit einer Einschränkung: Die im Inneren des Turmes frei hängenden, sich drehenden Körper konnten im Rahmen unserer Lehrveranstaltung leider nicht entsprechend mitverarbeitet werden.

Für die auf den folgenden Seiten dargestellten Ergebnisse aus dem Stabwerksprogramm war es wichtig, die Optik und grundlegenden Proportionen aus Tatlins Modellfotos nachzuempfinden. Die errechneten Ergebnisse beziehen sich zudem lediglich auf Belastungen aus dem Eigengewicht der Struktur; das durchgehend verwendete Material ist Stahl (ST52).

Das Gewicht der statisch wirksamen Struktur beläuft sich auf 116 400 Tonnen. Für die Knotenverbindungen wurden 10% aufgeschlagen, was letztlich zu einem Gesamtgewicht von ca. 128 000 Tonnen führte. Der immer wieder (optisch-konstruktive) strapazierte Vergleich mit dem hundert Meter niedrigeren Eiffelturm könnte also lauten, dass man für einen Tatlin-Turm knapp dreizehn von Eiffel hätte bauen können. Aber das war weder für Wladimir Tatlin, noch für die am Seminar beteiligten StudentInnen ein einschränkender Umstand.

Am Stabmodell zudem bemerkenswert ist die, durch den asymmetrischen Aufbau verstärkte Verformung und die ungleichmäßigen Auflagerdrücke im Bereich des ›Rückgrats‹. So kann in einem einzigen Punkt der (Spitzen-)Wert von knapp 200 000 kN als Auflagerdruck, am diagonal gegenüberliegenden Punkt ein Auflagerzug von etwa 60 000 kN abgelesen werden. Diese sehr unterschiedlichen Werte, vergleichsweise nah beieinander gelegen, hätten gerade im sumpfigen Boden St. Petersburgs für Schwierigkeiten gesorgt, und würden (selbst heute)

economical construction, are already known from architectural history. Even the massive 240 tons of steel used by Shukhov for his construction could only be attained thanks to Lenin's direct order to allocate material from army supplies in Smolensk (and even German Krupp steel is said to have been used). Vladimir Shukhov had, in 1919, the same year as Tatlin, presented a plan that stated that three towers with a height of 350 meters should be able to supply the whole Soviet Union with radio. Naturally, this estimate, which is quite similar to those Tatlin made for his monument, should have found favor with the Comintern. Both realistic and rather more fanciful visions of tower construction were not implemented in reality in the young Soviet Union of 1920 because of problems of production, which had already been identified by Karl Marx long ago.

nahe legen, die gesamte Konstruktion trotz allem visionären Überschwang nochmals zu überdenken.

Aus der Konstruktionsgeschichte sind die materiellen Schwierigkeiten von Wladimir Schuchov und seiner wunderbar sparsamen Konstruktion am Senderturm Šabolovka in Moskau bekannt.

Selbst die von Schuchov im Endeffekt benötigten 240 t Stahl konnten nur durch Lenins direkte Anweisung, Material aus Smolensker Heeresbeständen zur Verfügung zu stellen, eingesetzt werden (zusätzlich soll durch Lenin auch deutscher Kruppstahl zur Anwendung gekommen sein).

Wladimir Schuchov hatte 1919, also im gleichen Jahr wie Tatlin einen Plan vorgestellt, nach dem drei je 350 Meter hohe Sendetürme ausreichen würden, die gesamte Sowjetrepublik mit Radio zu versorgen. Eine Vorstellung, die sich inhaltlich ansatzweise mit Tatlins Programmierung seines Monuments deckt und der Komintern naturgemäß gefallen haben dürfte. Allein, die schon von Karl Marx beschworenen Produktionsumstände verhinderten auf vergleichsweise banale Art und Weise rationale wie irrationale Turmvisionen der jungen Sowjetunion anno 1920. Es war schlicht und einfach kein Material vorhanden.

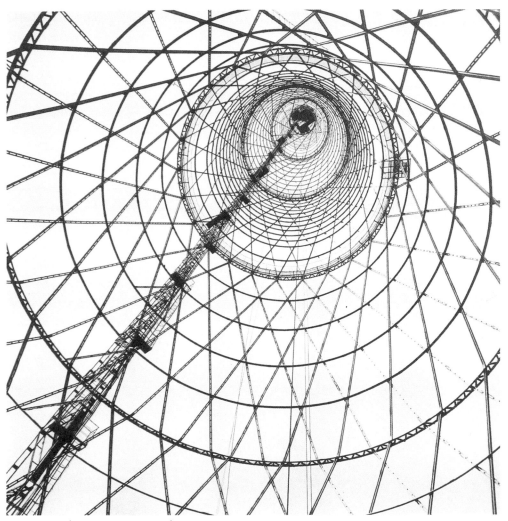

Interior view of *Shukhov Tower*, R. Graefe, 1989

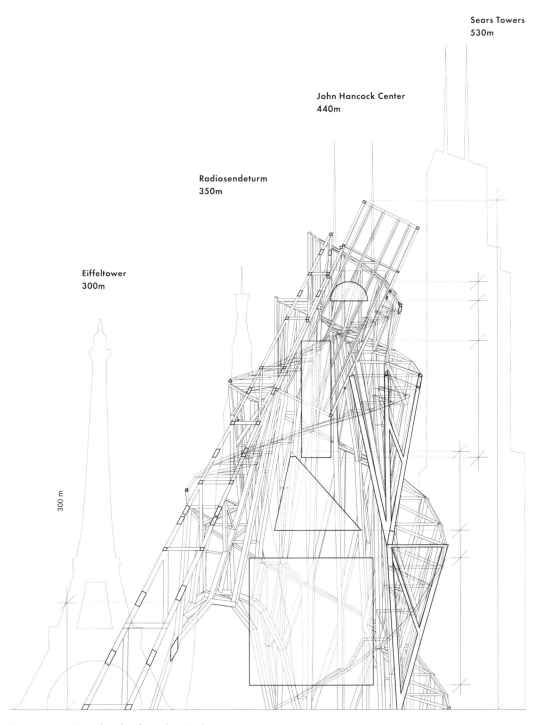

Sears Towers
530m

John Hancock Center
440m

Radiosendeturm
350m

Eiffeltower
300m

300 m

Monument section with scale-relation (seminar)

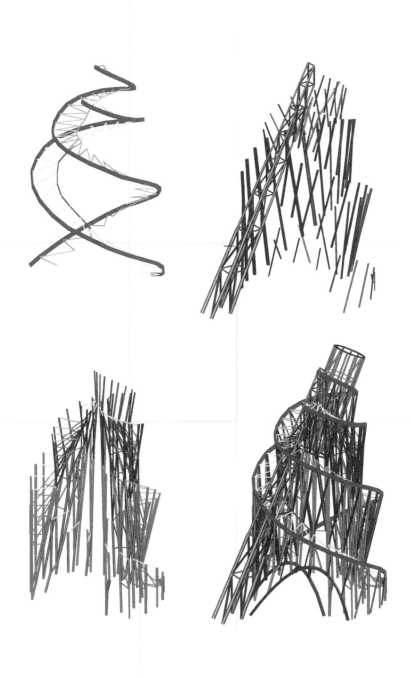

Construction diagram, structural elements (seminar)

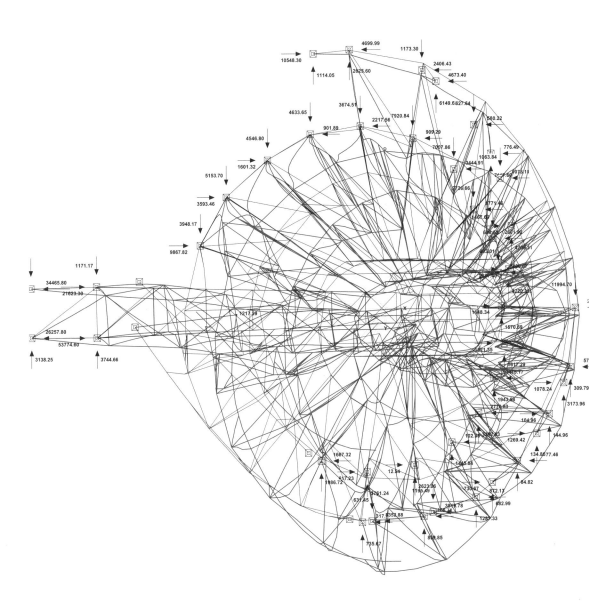

Structural deformation diagram, dead loads, top view (seminar)

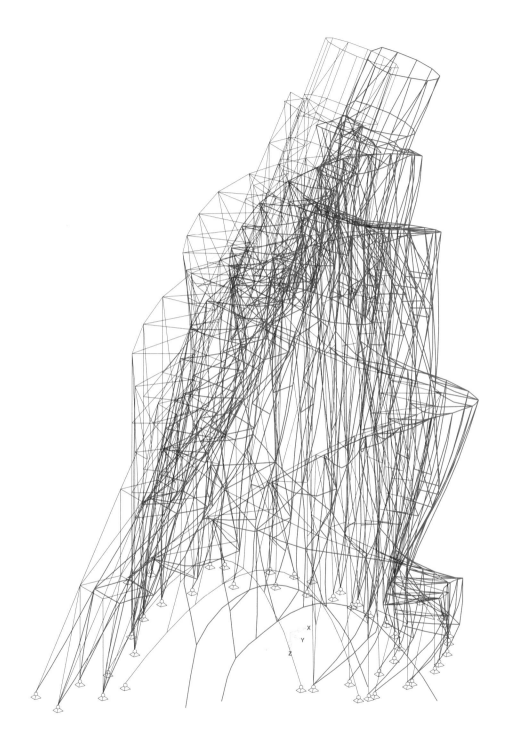

Structural deformation diagram, dead loads, axonometric view (seminar)

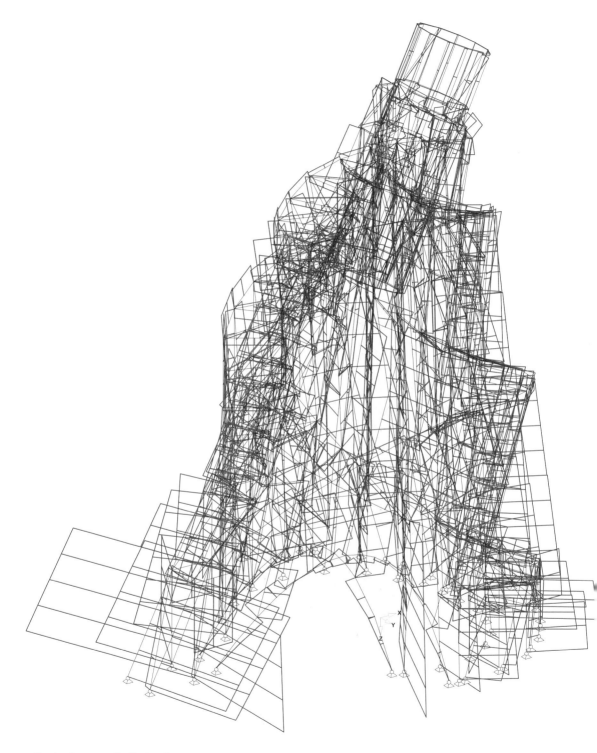

Structural moment distribution diagram

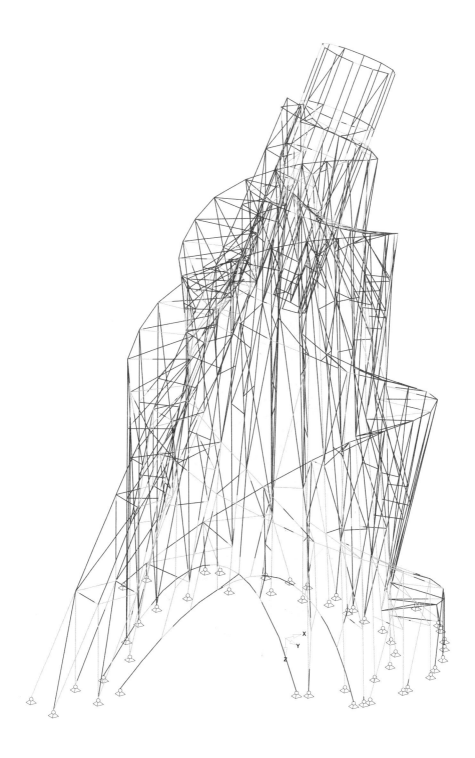

X
Y
Z

Structural stress diagram (seminar)

Tatlin-Tower, Istanbul (seminar)

Unbuildable Tatlin?!

Tatlin-Tower, Vienna (seminar)

Tatlin-Tower, Paris (seminar)

Tatlin-Tower, St. Petersburg (seminar)

Tatlin-Tower, St. Petersburg (seminar)

Tatlin-Tower, Gizeh (seminar)

Unbuildable Tatlin?!

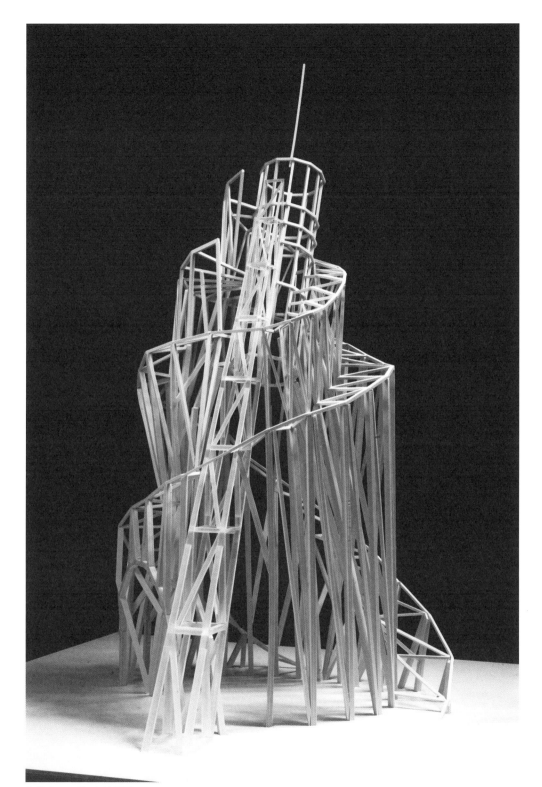

Tatlin-Tower, Model 1/500

Final Presentation   Abschlusspräsentation

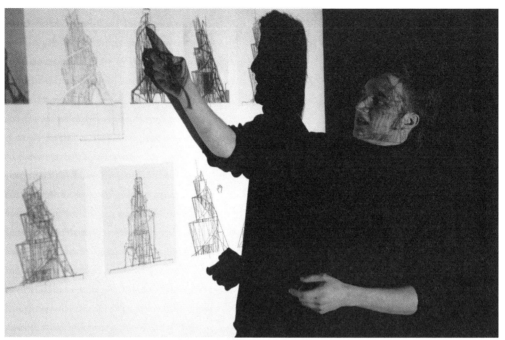

Alexander Diem

Giulio Polita, Wolf D. Prix, Liudmila and Vladislav Kirpichev

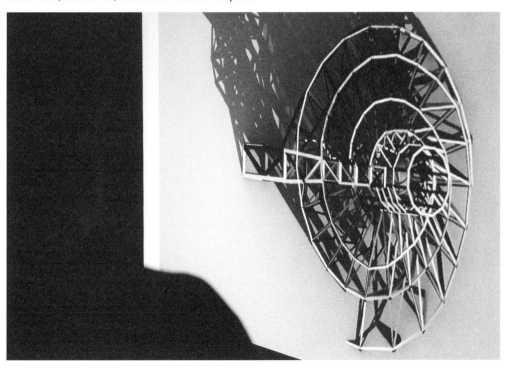

Tim Altenhof, Katharina Oechtering, Klaus Bollinger

Franz Gruber

Vladislav and Liudmila Kirpichev

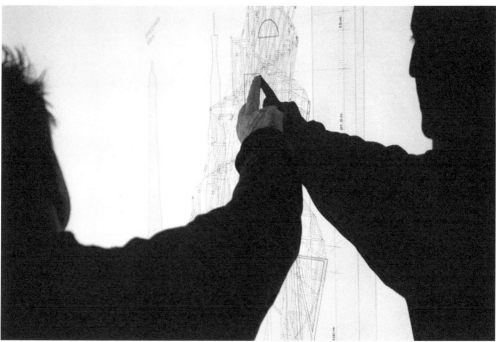

Final presentation   127

Vladimir Tatlin, Biography

Wladimir Tatlin, Biografie

Vladimir Tatlin, A. Rodchenko, 1917

Vladimir Yevgrafovich Tatlin loved mysti-fication—a fact which gave rise to more or less fortunate speculations concerning his biography. As the various accounts show, Tatlin's biography is a mixture of facts, anecdotes, claims and legends. The mystifi-cations in the meagre autobiographical information nevertheless seem to inten-tionally bridge the gap between reality and Tatlin's bold ideas of finishing the Tower of Babel or realizing the flight of Icarus. For Tatlin the mystified biography not only seemed to be "better" or "more interesting" but also closer to the very essence of his life and art.[1]

Already in his early years Tatlin's work was seen as an extraordinary pheno-menon, always giving rise to great hopes and expectations. People saw in him "some-body who knew about secrets" (Chlebnikow, 1916), a "seer, who has arrived at a clear dream" (Ehrenburg, 1922), a "terrific artist" (Majakowski, 1918), the "best artist in a Russia of workers and farmers" (Punin, 1920) or, especially strange, "a true saint of communist futurism, an enthusiastic fool for God with the face of a great martyr." (Efros, 1929).[2] Regarding his appearance Tatlin's contemporaries all described the "ugliness" of his facial features, his unsociability and his "secretiveness". Tatlin was extremely distrustful and therefore always anxious to hide things and to shield himself from alleged or real spying and curiosity by means of confusion. This fact led to a "reversed mystification"; no new infor-mation was created, it was mostly destroyed. While Tatlin's addiction for mystifications romanticized and colored his real biography, his almost morbid caginess caused real harm to it.[3]

Wladimir Yevgrafovich Tatlin liebte die Mystifikation; ein Umstand, der seit seinem Tod im Jahre 1953 einer ganzen Reihe von Forschern die Möglichkeit gab, sich hinsichtlich seiner Biografie in mehr oder weniger glücklichen Vermutungen zu ergehen. In Tatlins Biografie vermischen sich nach dem jeweiligen Wissensstand Fakten, Anekdoten, Behauptungen und Legenden. Die Mystifikationen in den spärlichen autobiografischen Angaben allerdings überbrücken scheinbar ganz bewusst die Kluft zwischen realer Existenz und Tatlins verwegenen Ideen, den baby-lonischen Turm fertig zu bauen oder den Flug des Ikarus zu verwirklichen. Die mysti-fizierte Biografie fand Tatlin offenbar nicht nur »besser« oder »interessanter«, sondern sie schien ihm auch dem wahren Kern seines Lebens und seiner Kunst genauer und vollständiger zu entsprechen.[1]

Schon in seinen jungen Jahren wurde Tatlins Schaffen als außerordentli-ches Phänomen begriffen und stets mit großen Hoffnungen und Erwartungen ver-knüpft. Man sah in ihm einen »um das Verborgene Wissenden« (Chlebnikow, 1916), einen »Seher, der bei einem klaren Traum angelangt ist« (Ehrenburg, 1922), einen »grandiosen Künstler« (Majakowski, 1918), den »besten Künstler im Arbeiter-und-Bauern-Russland« (Punin, 1920) oder, be-sonders kurios: »einen wahrhaft Heiligen des kommunistischen Futurismus, einen begeisterten Gottesnarr mit dem Antlitz eines Großmärtyrers« (Efros, 1929).[2] Bezüglich seiner Erscheinung erwähnen Tatlins Zeitgenossen einstimmig die »Häßlichkeit« seiner Gesichtszüge, seine Ungeselligkeit und seine »Geheimnis-krämerei«. Tatlin war unendlich misstrauisch

It is known for a fact that Vladimir Yevgrafovich Tatlin was born on December 28th, 1885 as the son of an engineer in Moscow. At the age of 13 he left home for family reasons and lived for some years as a casual labourer, went to Turkey and Syria as a shipboy and worked in the workshops of icon painters and stage designers. From 1905 to 1920 Tatlin studied at the art college in Penza, where he acquired the title of "Technical Draftsman". In February and March of 1914 Tatlin accompanied the exhibition of Russian folk art as a blind singer and bandura player; he then went to Paris to visit Picasso in his studio. In May of 1914 Tatlin organized an exhibition of material assemblages and "counter-reliefs", which was repeatedly shown during the following years. After the revolution Tatlin was actively engaged in building up and organizing a new art life; in 1917 he became a member of the "Left Block" and chairman of the "Young Federation" in the Union of Painters. In 1918 he took over the chair of the Moscow art council of the People's Commissariat for Education (NARKOMPROS) as well as the "Federation of Left Movements in the Arts" (until 1925); Tatlin became head of the department for material culture at the State Institute for Artistic Culture (GINCHUK) and worked in St. Petersburg (1919–1927) and Moscow (from 1927).

From 1934 on Tatlin was seen and criticized as representative of an "especially obvious and destructive formalism", while his work was constantly hindered by Soviet censorship. From 1940 until his death in 1953 Vladimir Tatlin had to rely on income from additional jobs such as stage designing.[4]

und deshalb stets bemüht, irgendetwas zu verbergen, zu verheimlichen und sich vor jeder wirklichen oder vermeintlichen Neugier und Bespitzelung durch Verwirrspiele zu schützen. Dieser Umstand führte zu einer »umgekehrten Mystifikation«: Es wurden keine Informationen erzeugt, sondern mehrheitlich vernichtet. Während Tatlins Hang zu Mystifikationen seine reale Biografie romantisierte und kolorierte, fügte seine beinah krankhafte Verschlossenheit ihr ernstlich Schaden zu.[3]

Als gesichert gilt, dass Wladimir Jefgrafowitsch Tatlin als Sohn eines Ingenieurs am 28. Dezember 1885 in Moskau geboren wurde. Im Alter von 13 Jahren verließ er aus familiären Gründen das Elternhaus und lebte einige Jahre von Gelegenheitsarbeiten, reiste als Schiffsjunge in die Türkei, nach Syrien und arbeitete in Werkstätten von Ikonenmalern und Bühnenbildnern. Von 1905 bis 1910 studierte Tatlin an der Kunstfachschule in Pensa, wo er den Titel eines »Fachzeichners« erwarb. Im Februar und März 1914 begleitete Tatlin als »blinder« Sänger und Bandura-Spieler die Ausstellung russischer Volkskunst nach Berlin; im Anschluss reiste er nach Paris und besuchte Picasso in seinem Atelier. Im Mai 1914 organisierte Tatlin eine Ausstellung seiner Materialsassemblagen und »Kontra-Reliefs«, die in den folgenden Jahren noch mehrfach gezeigt wurden.

Nach der Revolution beteiligte sich Tatlin aktiv an Aufbau und Organisation eines neuen Kunstlebens: 1917 wurde er Mitglied des »linken Blocks« und Vorsitzender der »jungen Föderation« innerhalb der neuen Fachunion der Maler. 1918 übernahm er den Vorsitz des Moskauer Kunstkollegiums des Volkskommissariats für

1, 2, 3 Anatoli Strigaljow, Tatlin – Leben, Werk, Wirkung;
DuMont, Cologne, 1993
4 cf. V. Tatlin's biography in Die grosse Utopie; Schirn
Kunsthalle Frankfurt, 1992

kulturelle Bildung (NARKOMPROS) sowie des »Verbandes linker Strömungen in der Kunst« (bis 1925); Tatlin wurde Leiter der Abteilung Materialkultur am Staatlichen Institut für künstlerische Kultur (GINCHUK) und arbeitete in St. Petersburg (1919–1927) und Moskau (ab 1927).

Ab 1934 wurde Tatlin als Vertreter eines »besonders offensichtlichen und schädlichen Formalismus« angesehen und kritisiert, während seine Arbeiten ständigen Behinderungen durch die sowjetische Zensur ausgesetzt waren. Ab 1940 bis zu seinem Tod 1953 war Wladimir Tatlin auf Nebenverdienste als Bühnenbildner an-gewiesen.[4]

1, 2, 3 Anatoli Strigaljow, Tatlin – Leben, Werk, Wirkung;
DuMont, Köln, 1993
4 Nach der Biografie V. Tatlins in Die grosse Utopie;
Schirn Kunsthalle Frankfurt, 1992

Letatlin (reconstruction) Jürgen Steger, 1991

Die Kunst ist tot
Es lebe die neue
Maschinenkunst
TATLINS

George Grosz and John Heartfild at the DADA-Exhibition, Berlin, 1920

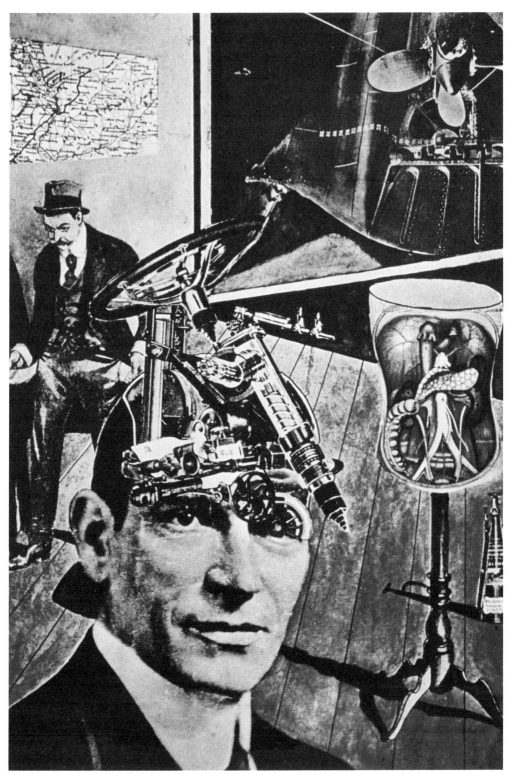

Tatlin at home, Raoul Hausmann, 1920

Monument to V. Tatlin, Dan Flavin, 1966–69

White Man Got No Dreaming, Tower (installation at the Biennale of Sydney, 2008), Michael Rakowitz, 2008

Vladimir Tatlin's Monument to the Third International put into music (installation in the tower of the centre d'art contemporain in Vassivière, France), Michel Aubry, 1921–2000

Fountain of Light, Ai Weiwei, steel and glass crystals on a wooden base, 2007

3G International, Aristarkh Chernyshev & Alexei Shulgin, fiberglass, duratrans, electronics

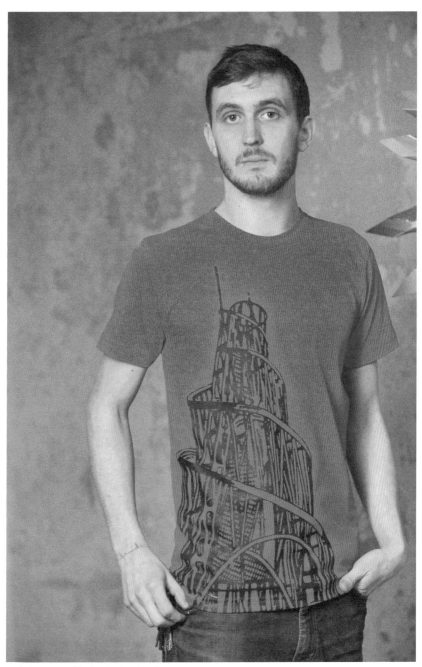

Tatlin's Tower T-shirt by TeeRex Syndicate

Contributors:

Klaus Bollinger
Structural Engineer, Germany
Professor at the University
of Applied Arts Vienna

Georg Glaeser
Professor at the University
of Applied Arts Vienna

Franz Gruber
Senior Scientist at the University
of Applied Arts Vienna

Florian Medicus
Architect, Austria
Senior Scientist at the University
of Applied Arts Vienna
and L.F. University, Innsbruck

Kurt Polanec
Structural Engineer,
Austria/Germany

Frank Werner
Architectural Theorist, Germany
Professor at the University Wuppertal
and TU Delft

Gabriele Werner
Art Historian, Austria
Professor at the University of Vienna

Image credits:

Frontispiece: Recreation of Tatlin's Tower in the Royal Academy's courtyard 2011/12. Photo: Courtesy of Francis Ware

p.6 *The Model of The Tower*, © Moderna Museet, Stockholm

p.9/53 Reconstruction of Tatlin's *Complex Corner Relief, 1915* by Martyn Chalk. Courtesy of Annely Juda Fine Art, London

p.11 *Tatlin Tower and Tectonic "Worldwind"*, Zaha Hadid, 1992. Courtesy of Zaha Hadid Architects London

p.17 BMW Welt: Interior view of the Double Cone made of steel and glass. © Ari Marcopoulos

South entrance of BMW Welt. A pedestrian bridge leads to the second level of the building, past the dynamic Double Cone. © Ari Marcopoulos

p.18 BMW Welt: Exploded view and isometric view of structural elements. © Bollinger+Grohmann

p.20 Rolex Learning Center, Lausanne, Rendering. © SANAA

Rolex Learning Center: Meshes of the finite element models of the big and the small shell. © Bollinger+Grohmann

Rolex Learning Center: Big shell after removing of the formwork. © Bollinger+Grohmann

p.23 Hungerburgbahn by Zaha Hadid, Hungerburg Station, Innsbruck. © Bollinger+Grohmann

p.24 Underground station roof, Piazza Garibaldi, Naples, Dominique Perrault, Italy 2007, evolutionary process. © Bollinger+Grohmann

Underground station roof, Piazza Garibaldi, Naples, Dominique Perrault, Italy 2007, competition model. © Bollinger+Grohmann

p.27 Sphere, Deutsche Bank, Mario Bellini, structure evolved through predefined architectural and structural fitness criteria, 2009–11. © Bollinger+Grohmann

p.30 *Shukhov Tower, 1922*, Alexander Rodchenko. © VBK, Wien, 2011

p.34 *Restaurant and landing over a slope*, Studio N. Ladovsky (WChUTEMAS), 1922; Drawing by Florian Unterberger, 2012

p.38 Reconstruction of Ivan Leonidow's Lenin-Institute (1927) 1992/93, University Stuttgart, IAG D.W. Schmidt, IDG M. Hechinger / Mutschelknaus, Voss. Photo by H.-J. Heyer

p.41 *Tatlin at work*, El Lissitzky, 1922. Courtesy of Grosvenor Gallery

p.42 *Tatlin's Tower*. Courtesy of Shchusev State Museum of Architecture, Moscow

p.47 Vladimir Tatlin and his assistants I.A. Meerzon and T.M. Shapiro constructing the first model for the *Monument to the Third International*, Petrograd, Soviet Union, 1920. Collection Centre Canadien d'Architecture / Canadian Centre for Architecture, Montréal

p.48 Vladimir Tatlin and his assistants I.A. Meerzon and T.M. Shapiro constructing the first model for the *Monument to the Third International*, Petrograd, Soviet Union, 1920. Collection Centre Canadien d'Architecture / Canadian Centre for Architecture, Montréal

p.50 Cover of the *Monument to the Third International*, Nicolai Punin, Petrograd, 1920

p.53/9 Reconstruction of Tatlin's *Complex Corner Relief, 1915*, Martyn Chalk. Courtesy of Annely Juda Fine Art, London

p.56 *The Confusion of Tongues*, Gustave Doré, 1865 (www.creationism.org/images)

p.59 *Solar Model*, Johannes Kepler, c.1597 (www.bru.hlphys.jku.at/surf/Kepler_Model.html)

Turris Babel, Livius Creyl and Athanasius Kircher, 1670

Later Model of the *Monument to the Third International*, Vladimir Tatlin, Paris, 1925

p.62 Model of the *Monument to the Third International*, Vladimir Tatlin (in front), Petrograd, 1920. Courtesy of David King Collection, London

p.64 *Design for a City with "Elevated Facades"*, Alexander Rodchenko, 1920

p.66 Drawing of Tatlin's Tower. Courtesy of Shchusev State Museum of Architecture, Moscow

p.70 *Spatial Construction No.12*, Alexander Rodchenko. c.1920, New York, Museum of Modern Art (MoMA). Plywood, open construction partially painted with aluminium paint, and wire, (61 × 83.7 × 47 cm). © 2012. Digital image, The Museum of Modern Art, New York/Scala, Florence

p.72 *Development of a Bottle in Space*, U. Boccioni, 1913, New York, The Metropolitan Museum of Art. © bpk | The Metropolitan Museum of Art

The Tower of Babel, Pieter Brueghel the Elder, 1563. © Kunsthistorisches Museum, Vienna

p.75 *The ArcelorMittal Orbit* by Anish Kapoor and Arup, Olympic Park, London, 2012. © Arup

p.86 Model of the *Monument to the Third International*, Petrograd, 1920. Courtesy of Shchusev State Museum of Architecture

p.88 Section of the *Monument to the Third International*, Vladimir Tatlin. Courtesy of Shchusev State Museum of Architecture

p.89 Section of the *Monument to the Third International*, Vladimir Tatlin. Courtesy of Shchusev State Museum of Architecture

p.93 *G. Eiffel et un autre homme debout devant un des piliers de la Tour Eiffel le 18 Juillet 1887*, Louis-Emile Durandelle, Paris Musée d'Orsay, don de Mme Bernard Granet et ses enfants et de Mme Solange Granet, 1981

p.109 Interior view of Shukhov Tower. © Rainer Graefe, 1989

p.124–127 All images © Reiner Zettl

p.128 *Vladimir Tatlin*, A. Rodchenko. Courtesy of David King Collection, London

p.131 *Letatlin* (reconstruction) Jürgen Steger, 1991. © Zeppelin Museum Friedrichshafen-Technik und Kunst

p.132 George Grosz and John Heartfield at the DADA exhibition, Berlin, 1920. Courtesy of Akademie der Bildenden Künste Berlin

p.133 *Tatlin at home*, Raoul Hausmann, 1920. © Moderna Museet, Stockholm

p.134 *Monument to V. Tatlin*, Dan Flavin, 1966–69. Courtesy of National Gallery of Australia, Canberra. © Dan Flavin, licensed by VBK, Austria

p.135 *White Man Got No Dreaming, Tower* (installation at the Biennale of Sydney, 2008), Michael Rakowitz, demolished Aboriginal houses, wires, copper pipe, and wood, 640 × 336 cm, 2008

p.136 *Vladimir Tatlin's Monument to the Third International put into music*, Michel Aubry, 1921–2000, installation in the tower of the centre d'art contemporain in Vassivière, France. Photo by Frédéric Delpech

p.137 *Fountain of Light*, Ai Weiwei, steel and glass crystals on a wooden base, (h)700 × 529 × 400 cm, 2007. © Ai WeiWei

p.138 *3G International*, Aristarkh Chernyshev & Alexei Shulgin, fiberglass, duratrans, electronics. Courtesy of XL Gallery Moscow

p.139 *Tatlin's Tower*. © TeeRex Syndicate and Greg Lafaro